Real Estate Agent Success for Beginners

The Realtor's Sales Guide to Marketing &
Lead Generation via YouTube, Phone Scripts,
and Other Strategies for Closing the Deal

David Harris

Table of Contents

Introduction

Do you want to be a successful real estate agent? Apart from gaining proper education, it is also necessary for you to develop some introductory skills designed to help you succeed in this industry. Note that this type of job requires you to have inherent skills and hone them so that you can use them to succeed and attain professional growth.

You also have to know how you can quickly transfer your present skills to your new line of work. This is especially true if you are still a newbie in the world of real estate marketing. Apart from that, you should be willing to expand on your skillset. The first thing that you should do is to evaluate your current skillset. Determine the essential skills that an aspiring real estate agent must have. How many of these skills do you already have? What are the skills that you still need to hone or acquire?

Here are some introductory skills you have to develop if you want to be successful as a real estate agent:

Excellent Communication Skills

The way you communicate with your clients contributes a lot to closing a deal. It can serve as your bridge when connecting to not only property buyers but also sellers. It is the reason why mastering various communication channels is necessary for beginners like you.

By boosting your communication skills, you can easily and quickly deliver pertinent information to your clients. It is an important skill for you to master, as it can help you achieve almost every task that you need to do, including explaining the buying process to buyers, negotiating offers, and marketing to prospects through your blog, website, or social media.

Among the most vital communication skills you need to possess and hone for success are:

- Writing and verbal skills

- Active listening skills

- Interpersonal communication skills

- Selling, negotiation, and networking skills

- Ability to read body language

It is also crucial to know how to detect the specific method of communication that each client prefers. Ask your present and prospective clients how they intend to communicate with you. It could be through text, phone, in-person meetings, emails, or any other method they find comfortable. With the different modes of communication preferred by different clients, you may also need to be proficient in using various communication channels.

Ability to Adapt to New Technology

Your chosen job requires you to stay in an ever-evolving industry. It is the reason why the technology and tools used to navigate the real estate industry tend to change constantly. With that in mind, you also need to have the skill to adapt to this new technology and learn to use it to your advantage.

Fortunately, most of the tech-based changes promote more convenience for both agents and clients. It means that investing your energy and time learning the basics of using something new will benefit you for a long time.

People Skills

Your clients will always be your main priority once you decide to take up a career in the real estate industry. Because of that, constantly remind yourself that you need to integrate a personal touch in each of your attempts to build a strong relationship with them. One way to do that is to remember the special milestones in their lives, like their birthdays.

Also, remember that being a real estate agent means that you will be dealing and working with a lot of people. You will be dealing with home inspectors, attorneys, loan officers, and other professionals involved in a real estate transaction. Honing your people skills, therefore, is extremely important to flourish in your career.

Apart from building a connection with your clients, you also need to use your people skills to connect with other professionals. This skill is what will help you network and connect with resources and a group or community of people necessary for your professional growth.

Time Management Skills

Time management is another introductory skill that will help you to launch your career as a realtor. By honing this skill, you can figure out exactly how you will spend your time every day and week. You will need to have full control of your schedule and allocate your time wisely. Your time management skills will also make you more responsible about the way you consume your time. You will start allocating enough time for certain activities or transactions.

Apart from that, your efficiency in managing your time will impress your clients. You will never miss out on appointments with clients and other industry professionals. Your time management skills will also let you accomplish all your tasks on time.

Marketing and Negotiation Skills

You have to become an excellent marketer and negotiator, too. Negotiation is always a vital aspect in the lives of real estate agents, so brush up on your skills and knowledge in this area. Learn how to scrutinize even the smallest details in a real estate transaction. That way, you can negotiate better, especially when dealing with a client.

Hone your marketing skills as well since you will need to market your services every day. Understand everything about marketing, particularly those methods that most marketers use today. These include social media, branding, and email marketing. Also, be willing to adapt to any change in marketing in the future too. This will help to promote your business.

Integrity/Honesty

Your integrity/honesty is also a strong foundation for your success. It is an introductory trait and skill you have to showcase even if you are still a beginner. Develop your integrity by ensuring you do not do anything that may cause you to look unethical, immoral, and dishonest. Never do anything that will tarnish your name and reputation. Harness your integrity and honesty as it is vital in building a good client base capable of presenting great testimonies of the successful deals you have closed recently.

Deep Knowledge about the Industry

Your knowledge about the real estate industry also needs to be in-depth before you ever start working as an agent. Remember that some potential clients have no idea about the steps they should take when investing in a home or property. This makes your in-depth knowledge about this field significant.

You can use it to teach your clients everything they need to know about property investments. You may even offer hands-on guidance and assistance to make the experience rewarding, pleasant, and comfortable for both you and your clients.

Your knowledge about the industry can also build your credibility. It will position you as a valuable source of information. This is especially true if you publicize your knowledge on your website and other online channels.

Leadership

Good leadership skills can also help you succeed. Develop your ability to lead people to the point when you can motivate them to do something while allowing them to commit to your ideas and ideas.

Strategies to Become a Successful Real Estate Agent

Apart from honing the qualities and skills mentioned above, it is also crucial to learn the ins and outs of the industry. Learn about the different strategies that can drive you toward success. For instance, you can implement a small business system to improve your life and the lives of your future and present clients.

Some other strategies for success that you can use include:

- Set realistic goals – Set a target, especially in terms of your sales and income. By setting your goals and targets, you can easily keep track of and measure your progress. Make sure that the goals you have set are not only specific but that they are also measurable, realistic, actionable, and time-bound. Having such a goal is a sure-fire way to lock in your desired success.

- Act like a winner starting from day one – Your first few days as a licensed realtor may be a period of adjustment for you, but you still have to show your confidence whenever you do your job. Be confident in what you do so you can show everyone that you have what it takes to be a winner right from your first day of work. This helps clients to trust you.

Remember that, as a realtor, it is necessary to sell yourself and your skills, not just properties. Work on making connections and building trust by letting everyone know that you are genuinely confident in your knowledge and skills. By acting as a knowledgeable and expert realtor, you will certainly attract clients who want to sell or buy properties with or from you.

- Secure clients – Learn and master every method that you can use to secure and build lifelong relationships with clients. Even at the start of your career, you already need to have a marketing campaign set up in place. Secure clients by taking advantage of automated marketing, too. Master both old-school marketing methods and new and advanced technology. Mix them up in your campaign to reach a broader customer base.

Should You Be a Listing Agent or a Buying Agent?

Being a listing agent actually has a lot more perks than working as a buying agent. If you want to succeed in this industry, then you may want to focus more on becoming a listing agent. You may find it easier to find leads if you decide to be a buying agent, but prioritizing listings can greatly impact your career in the real estate industry in a positive way.

As a beginner, your mindset may focus on building your reputation by working primarily with buyers. Eventually, though, you will have to start developing your own listings – after which you can start climbing to the industry's pinnacle position known as that of a listing agent.

If you want to build long-term success, a superior quality of life, and a flourishing and profitable career, then you have to set goals to be part of the elite group – the listing agents who consist of just 5 percent or less of real estate agents. Some perks of being part of this group are:

- Provides multiple income streams – Apart from generating interest, listings can also result in additional business and transactions. Right from the moment you announced a listing through various means – offline or online, expect to receive emails, texts, and calls from active buyers and neighbors.

  You may even get inquiries from those who just drove around the neighborhood trying to establish if it suits them, as well as from people who plan to live in that area. All of these inquiries and leads will represent your present and future opportunities in the industry, and they may only arise if you announce a listing that has your name on it.

- Serves as a business multiplier – The good thing about being a listing agent is that it can multiply your business several times over. Any listing agent you talk to will surely confirm that fact, proving that a single listing is usually equivalent to more than just a single sale. With that, it is safe to assume that it can help you have a flourishing and profitable career as a realtor. People will see your name.

- Gives you complete control of your time – Being a listing or seller's agent offers an opportunity to create your own timeline for appointments, inspections, showings, and open houses.

  It is different from when you are a buying agent that often requires you to spend even your nights and weekends with clients. The reason is that your schedule will usually be based on their free time. Going the listing agent route lets you set your own normal schedule. Just stick to your schedule the best way you can to show your professionalism.

- Comes with a legally binding contract – This means that a seller is obliged to work with you by contract. The seller can't ditch you just because they found another agent to work with. Every time you put your signature on a listing agreement with a specific seller, you can expect the document to be legally binding.

- With that, you will be the one who has the power to release them in case they go for other agents. You can even receive a referral bonus or any other agreed compensation based on the time and effort you put into the contract.

- Provides several promotional opportunities – Even a single listing can provide you with a reason to promote, advertise, or grab the attention of leads or prospects that you can successfully convert into actual clients.

Moreover, it is possible to spread the word of how successful you are once you have sold your listing. You can start establishing a connection with those around the neighborhood, and on social media and increase your entire sphere of influence. You can expect that to happen, especially once they know how good you are.

- Allows you to work with a team of agents for free – Right after posting or announcing your listing, you can expect the other realtors or agents around the area to begin working on your behalf, too. The good news is that most of them do not require you to pay unless they provide you with a buyer.

When that happens, you will not be the one to shoulder the payment. You can expect them to be paid through the commission structure by the actual seller you are working with.

Those are just a few of the many perks of working as a listing agent. However, note that regardless of the route you chose, the real estate agent job, in general, is already very rewarding. Just ensure that you hone your skills and gather as much information as possible about the best strategies you can implement to become successful.

Now that you know the basics, it is time to learn more about the other things you can do to attain success, even if you are still a beginner. Start making your mark in the industry with all the information and guidance provided by this book. Remember that working as a top-selling realtor requires an excellent work ethic, and you can develop that with proper guidance.

At the end of this book, you will know exactly how to attain success in this industry. You can even build the required tenacity to pursue each lead while hustling to market the properties of your clients aggressively.

The focus of this reading material is not putting in too much of your time and effort but learning to work smartly. In other words, you will learn how to put the right amount of time and effort into closing deals and avoid those activities that can sap your energy and waste your time.

Chapter 1

Choosing the Right Company to Deal With

A major contributor in your attempt to attain a flourishing career in the real estate industry is the real estate company or broker you are affiliated with or working for. It is the reason why you have to take your time deciding on the specific company to work with.

At the start of your real estate career, make it a point to research the most prominent real estate companies and brokerage firms at this present time. Working with the best one, combined with your lucrative professional strategies and skills, is a sure-fire way to build a prominent reputation in this industry.

Why Do You Need to Choose a Good Real Estate Company?

A real estate firm or company refers to a brokerage firm, either local or national, that hires licensed real estate agents – the ones who will be representing local sellers and buyers. If you are just getting started on your career, then the right broker can lead you to success.

Remember that signing up with a real estate company or brokerage firm is a requirement for those who intend to become an agent – that is on top of meeting state education requirements and passing the licensure exam.

Before you ever get the chance to sell your first property, it is a must to look for a real estate company capable of suiting your requirements. Opt for one that can truly make you feel confident. Find a good company that will act as your valuable resource when you are still starting out. They should be well-versed and adept at real estate properties around the neighborhood and know exactly what it takes to close good and profitable deals.

A good brokerage firm also knows about listings. They are experienced in identifying genuine sellers and buyers and have the expertise to sort out the information provided by the internet, which means they also know what advice to ignore. Most of these firms have a stable network of like-minded people and professionals as well.

However, you can't just choose to work in any firm that offers you a position. You need to sort out and narrow down all your options. Take your time figuring out which one suits your needs and can give you the following benefits:

- Immediate recognition and market awareness, leading to a higher number of prospective sellers and buyers
- Access to valuable business resources and marketing tools
- A stable source of potential customers and referrals
- High and stable earning potential
- Professional and effective mentoring and training
- Numerous networking opportunities
- Is aware of every legal documentation needed for property transactions, thereby eliminating worry and stress
- Increases visibility and traffic since the company already has a strong network of collaboration composed of numerous other real estate brokerage firms as well as their buyers

All these benefits can lead you in the right direction, allowing you to achieve the personal and financial goals you have set for yourself as well as enjoy an impressive career and professional growth.

Closing Deals in Both the Buyer's and Seller's Market

Ask realtors about the hardest and most challenging part of their journey when they were still starting, and they will say that it is actually not passing the state exam or attending pre-licensing classes. It is finding clients in both the buyer's and sellers' markets. Obviously, those who have large markets and broad social networks are the ones guaranteed to have better marketing potential and opportunities.

You can further boost your chance of finding clients and closing deals whether you are in the buyers' and sellers' market by working for a company that implements robust marketing techniques. How will you know if you are dealing with such a company? Here are some of the components and offers you need to look for:

Proper Training

Of course, as a beginner, an excellent training program can help you a lot. You need to work for a company that can provide you with the best training program – one that focuses more on procuring business and improving your marketing prowess.

Spend time assessing the training programs offered by the real estate companies you are considering working for. Assess them based on the following information:

- What kind of training does the company offer for new realtors or agents? – If no training or mentorship program is in place, then it may not be the ideal place to hang your license in.
- Is there a designated trainer? – It could be that the firm has an experienced agent or the broker himself, who serves as the mentor for newly recruited agents.
- Do you have to attend regular classes?
- Are there regional or local training sessions for newly recruited agents if the company is a

franchise? – If that is the case, then who will shoulder the training fee?

- Is there someone from the company who can offer assistance every time you need help as a beginner?
- Does the company offer advanced sales skills training? When and how do they offer such training sessions?
- Do they support licensing and continuing education?
- Do they offer employee-to-employee mentorship?
- Is the firm responsible for securing licenses and fees? Or is it the responsibility of agents to pay for the additional resources they need on their own?
- How much guidance can you expect from the company, especially during your first few years as an agent?

Ask about the background of the specific person or group of people who will provide you the training and assistance you need, too. Yes, you are already a licensed realtor, but you will still need to be guided during the first few times you will be evaluating a property, listing it for sale, and negotiating and structuring complex selling and purchase transactions accurately. You should, therefore, hone the necessary skills through proper training.

Study how they recruit, train, and initiate their licensed agents. It is a good sign if the company offers a professional training approach and provides a good training and initiation curriculum when they partner you with a mentor licensee. The firm should also provide easy and sufficient access to the actual broker in case of sticky situations.

Moreover, the training sessions need to be designed to help new licensees, like you, to become successful. They should focus on the following – all of which can guide you toward successfully closing deals.

- Nurturing prospects and leads – The real estate industry will always operate on a numbers game. This means that realtors live or die depending on how effective they are in following up on prospects and leads.

  The entire real estate buying and selling process can also be long and tedious. Each prospect has a unique requirement every time they search for property. With that in mind, the key to closing deals is to receive proper training in lead nurturing, engaging prospects, and thinking ahead – all of which can help to add funds to the pipeline.

- Basic communication skills – Even if you think you are already adept in clearly writing property descriptions and communicating with people personally or via the phone, you still need to be constantly trained. You need to constantly practice and hone your communication skills, especially because your job will always involve delivering and stating a specific message.

  Go for a company or brokerage firm with people who are willing to train their agents to communicate well. They should motivate them to put their message into practice. The company needs to have a program in place that continues to train agents, like yourself, to develop the best skills necessary to interact with clients and leads more effectively.

- How to use and access the latest technology – This should form part of the training regardless of whether you are tech-savvy or not. Nowadays, technology makes it a lot easier for realtors to showcase their properties to leads and clients.

  The problem is that technology is also kind of intimidating and complicated, especially if your knowledge about it is scarce. It is why you need to work for a company that can teach you the basics of all the latest technology that you can use in this industry.
  Through proper training, you can master the basics of using technology to your best advantage, rather than being intimidated by it.

- How to use MLS listings – Nowadays, you can see a lot of people conducting their searches for homes online. When doing an online search, there is a possibility that the details and information they gathered came from an MLS (multiple listing system).

  Even if you are already adept in using technology, particularly that which can assist you in your career, you may never have experienced using an

MLS database yet. It is important to learn about this system during your training as it can help you keep up with other agents who already know how to make the most of it.

A lot of agents are now using it whenever they need to post a listing or check out other properties around a specific area. If you are still unfamiliar with this system, then getting trained on how to use it is definitely a big help for you.

- Marketing – Of course, you need all the support you can get when it comes to marketing and promotions. Find a company that can give you adequate training in this area. You should receive training about both the traditional and modern forms of marketing as well as local market trends.

Modern technology may have made marketing somewhat more complicated, but note that its principles still stay the same. Therefore, your chosen firm should, focus on training agents in how to market themselves as well as their listings. They should be able to provide formal training, especially about negotiating and sales techniques.

This will arm agents with the skills and knowledge necessary to bring themselves to the attention of a lot of prospects and create profitable leads. If possible, there should also be a mentorship program facilitated by senior agents as they are the ones who already know the ins and outs of the industry.

- Effective time management and scheduling – The training also needs to cover topics related to effective time management and scheduling. Remember that both these skills are essential when it comes to closing deals, even if you are still a beginner.

As a new real estate agent, though, acquiring your desired number of prospects and leads may not be attainable yet. In that case, you may start thinking that time management and proper scheduling are unnecessary. However, you still need to hone those skills through proper training as, eventually, you will get busier and busier.

By that time, you will have to watch your schedules more closely. By receiving proper training on scheduling and time management, you can develop a solid framework that you can follow and grow into.

Apart from the above-mentioned vital components of training, you also have to find out whether you will receive ongoing training once the company employs you. Remember that getting your license is a time-consuming and intensive process. It is a journey you have to study and prepare for over a long time, months even. Passing the exam and getting your complete license will be a source of relief and accomplishment for you.

However, note that having your license does not necessarily mean you are already an expert in the industry. You still need ongoing training. Taking that into consideration, determine if the company where you are planning to apply has a program set in place for ongoing training and education.

Together with continuing education, you need to revisit what you have learned previously every now and then while brushing up on your knowledge regarding new trends and updates in the industry. This can contribute to your professional growth and development.

Exterior and Interior Amenities and Facilities

Apart from the training, you also have to check the in-house and off-site amenities and facilities provided by the firm as this plays a major role in attracting clients once you start working there. Though it is true that you should avoid judging a book by its cover, you should still not ignore your first impression upon seeing the firm for the first time.

If the facility's atmosphere and aesthetics are not comfortable or attractive enough, then it is highly likely that prospective clients will perceive the firm in that way, too. It can hurt your chance of successfully closing a deal. Once you set foot on the company premises, spend time inspecting the place, including the entrances, signs, parking choices, as well as overall look.

Consider the neighborhood and actual location of the company, too. Get an idea about the actual size of the firm as you will actually discover a few pros and cons to getting affiliated with small single-man shops, mid-sized ones, and huge establishments.

When it comes to the interior, inspect how clean it is first. Check the arrangement of the offices and workspaces, too. Do you find its foyer comfortable, uncluttered, and welcoming? Does the company have semi-private and private areas that you and your future clients can easily access to discuss needs and requirements and sign contracts? Do you find the noise level inside the office okay? Do they greet you and other visitors right after entering the door?

Find answers to all those questions and visualize yourself as the client walking into the office for the first time. Determine if the place is welcoming enough with staff treating guests and clients nicely and taking the time to greet them.

If you feel good and welcomed, then expect prospective clients to feel the same way too. It is a plus point if you are looking for a company that can truly help you boost your sales.

Available Resources

Determine the specific resources that will be made available to you upon getting hired. Find out if such resources can help you do all your professional duties and responsibilities with flying colors. For instance, you may want to know whether you will be receiving a shared workspace and phone first or whether you will have your own workspace, desk, and admin support.

One thing to note about real estate companies and brokers is that they provide various levels of workspace, including shared desks and private offices. The one that will be provided to a particular agent will depend on the license he is holding – whether he is a salesperson or a broker.

Factors like seniority and annual sales will also affect the resources that will be made available for you. Find out if such resources are included in the policy manual. If that is the case, then request a copy.

However, if you plan to work as an independent contractor, then be prepared to shoulder most, if not all, office expenses. These include long-distance phone charges, postage costs, individual publicity, and office/desk/cubicle rental, among many others. Check whether the resources that the company provides are the exact ones you need to win clients.

Online Presence

You also have a better chance of closing deals if you work for a company that has a strong online presence. In that case, it helps if the company has its own established website. Take the time to check and scrutinize the website first. When visiting the site, check if it can give you in-depth information regarding the brokerage firm, including how it started, its mission statement, staff, sponsorships, awards, and professional affiliations.

Apart from figuring out whether the website is chock-full of relevant information, assess how user-friendly it is, too. The site should be well-organized and feature an appealing design – one that will attract leads and potential clients.

As much as possible, the listings posted on the site should contain present data and high-quality photos. They should also provide virtual tour options. All these elements will encourage prospective clients to stay on the site and grab more information about what the company offers.

Moreover, you will know that the firm has a good website capable of attracting clients if it can encourage them to communicate with or contact the firm to establish business relationships. It indicates that it has a strong tool that significantly enhances its online presence.

Marketing and Advertising Efforts

Determine the specific manner through which the firm markets itself around the neighborhood through various traditional means, like real estate publications, billboards, TV and radio ads, and local newspapers. By gathering these vital marketing and advertising details, you can grasp the company's professional policies and regulations.

You will also learn about the reputation of the firm and the nature of the real estate agents and other related professionals who are under them. You also need to get to know more about the company's marketing and advertising efforts as this information will give you an idea of whether they are in line with your goals of attracting quality clientele and closing deals.

Weighing All Your Options

As mentioned earlier, there are numerous real estate companies offering new agents a place where they can comfortably and confidently put their skills and knowledge to good use. This is especially true if you include related areas and fields, such as lenders, inspectors, and appraisers.

However, your ultimate goal is most likely working for a legitimate and stable company, which facilitates the selection, selling, and buying of real estate properties. Fortunately, your options are also wide and varied in that case. Just make sure to decide on a specific niche beforehand.

You need to have a clear idea of the specific type of company that will guide and help you toward attaining your goals. In terms of the types of company, your options often include the following:

Mom-and-Pop Company

This first category of a real estate company refers to one where the owner or broker still lists and sells real estate. In other words, the owner has no separate manager yet. It would be a great choice for you if you would like to work in a company with less than 20 agents only and is not a part of a franchise.

This type is actually favorable and beneficial for beginners like you because fewer agents means that your training will also be prioritized. The owner or broker will be able to focus on motivating each agent and inspiring them to work hard.

Moreover, the entire atmosphere in the workplace will most likely be positive and intimate instead of being messy, too competitive, and pressuring. It could be a great place to start your career and acquire knowledge, though you have to make sure that you will receive proper training if you get hired here.

Large Independent Company

There is also what we categorize as a large and independent real estate company. It does not belong to any franchise organization. It works under sole ownership with a huge number of agents – at least a hundred or two hundred. Some of these independent companies even employ more than two thousand agents.

This would be the perfect company for you if what you are looking for is a stable company that has a significant flow of money. With its huge number of agents, it is also possible that it has a huge market share, which is the reason why it has a stable flow of income. Even better, it offers the chance to funnel back the earned funds to the real estate agents in the local market and advertising.

Being a large and independent company, they also want to focus their money, resources, effort, and energy on the specific market they intend to cover. Their goal is to be a leader in the industry. If you are still a beginner, there is a tendency for you to get lost within the organization unless your manager is someone who is hands-on and wants to prioritize training new agents.

Still, being added into the mix of the right company, one that is genuinely after your growth, will make you feel like you have a large family willing to help you improve, especially as far as your career is concerned.

Franchise

You can also work for companies that belong to a franchise. Among the most famous franchises in the real estate industry at present are Keller Williams, Better Homes & Gardens, Realty One, Coldwell Banker, and Century 21. By getting into any of these famous franchises, an independent company or a mom-and-pop can no longer consider itself as independent.

There are several advantages when you get employed into real estate companies that are part of a franchise. For one, it allows agents to take full advantage of the company's power in terms of national exposure.

Aside from that, a famous franchise can give its people proper and adequate training and education. Note that most of these franchise companies are the ones who have already earned an excellent reputation in the industry, so you have a hundred percent guarantee that you will learn a lot from them. Such an excellent reputation also results in name recognition and higher perceived value, among many other benefits.

Working in this type of company has its downside, though — one of which would be the fact that there will be a specific percentage of your commission that will immediately go to the franchise's national advertising and marketing budget. It may eat up a chunk of your profit.

However, some realtors still say that the amount taken from their profit for advertising and promotion comes back several-fold. The reason is that the kind and quality of business and transaction they will be getting are superior compared to others. It is something that they can't get if they do not belong to a franchise.

Discount Broker

Another category of real estate company where new agents, like you, can test their mettle and learn is the discount broker. Some franchises even solely focus on this type of business. The discount broker operates by providing limited services to sellers. The fact that their marketing is limited also means that they will be charging lower fees to their sellers compared to other types of companies.

For instance, if a specific market's average commission is around 5%, the discount broker can only have a commission of around 2 to 3 percent. This type of business tries to attract sellers using something different from marketing or the market share – and that is purely based on price. It is what this category mainly focuses on.

To give you an idea of how it works, it would be like deciding whether you should go to a clinic that charges its patients less but offers fewer services or a doctor whose specialization is in the specific ailment that you would like to cure. The discount broker that we are talking about here operates similarly to that clinic, while the full-service broker that charges a higher commission is the doctor with a specialization.

100% Real Estate Company

This is another profitable type of company where you can offer your skills and expertise as a real estate agent and get paid in return. To gain a full understanding of how this 100% real estate company functions, it is necessary to know exactly how realtors or real estate agents get paid. In that case, remember that each transaction in this industry comes with two sides – listing and selling.

The agent and office that took a certain buyer to a particular property encompass the selling side of the transaction. The listing side, on the other hand, refers to the office that did the property listing. Based on that premise, the 100% commission will be split in half – 50% of it for the selling side while the remaining half will be for the listing side. The real estate agent of each side shares the portion with the broker.

For instance, if you receive a $5,000 commission for a certain transaction, then the listing and selling offices will receive $2,500 each. If the commission split agreed upon by the agents and the broker is 50-50, then expect both agents to receive $1,250 each while the broker for every office will receive the remaining $1,250.

Based on that principle, it is safe to say that the 100% model functions on the scenario that the broker will receive payment from the rent charged to every agent. In this case, working as an agent for this company means you will be paying the broker a specific amount monthly regardless of whether you earned any money for that month or not.

You will also be the one who will be shouldering your own expenses, including advertising and supplies. This is not going to be the case if you choose to work for the other types of businesses mentioned earlier, so it is important to weigh up your options and think twice before deciding to apply to any of the 100% real estate companies that are still in operation right now.

Other Possible Classifications

Apart from the already mentioned types of real estate companies, you can also find other possible classifications and hybrids. You may decide on the company to work for from these classifications:

- Residential – In this classification, agents, realtors, and brokers work along with sellers and buyers in buying and selling resold and new private homes. The majority of the transactions in this field actually belong to residential. You can also find sub-specialists here who only work with sellers, buyers, first-time buyers of properties, relocations, and seniors.

- Commercial – You can also find real estate companies that focus more on commercial properties. Such companies work primarily with businesses to identifying, sell or purchase land or property that is perfect for commercial purposes. These include retail, light industrial, restaurant, and office properties.

  If you intend to get involved in this type of company, then remember that commercial deals require more engagement and involvement compared to residential ones. They also tend to take longer compared to other transactions. Aside from identifying properties, most agents and brokers in this field are also expected to offer assistance in zoning, financing, permitting, feasibility studies, and development.

- Industrial – The industrial classification is actually a unique subset of commercial properties needing a certain set of skills and knowledge as well as specialized relationships. If your chosen company focuses more on the industrial spectrum, then your clients may be looking for not only the perfect geographical location but also a locale capable of offering an appropriate labor pool, governmental relationship, regulatory environment, and tax structure.

  Therefore, the agents and brokers in this company should develop a smooth and convenient way for the client to attain the approval of seller, buyer, state and local government, and community leaders.

- Land – This classification covers those brokerage firms that primarily specialize in spotting and finding raw land that can be used by commercial clients or home builders for development. Working in this company requires you to gather expertise in things like the zoning process. Moreover, you need to gain knowledge of local government regulations and establish a positive relationship with the municipal authority.

- Investor – This firm focuses more on establishing work relationships with sole investors and investment groups. The goal of this company is to assist clients in locating income-producing properties, such as retail centers (ex. strip malls), apartment buildings, and rental homes.

  It is also crucial to know about the area surrounding the property, the unique selling feature/s of the property compared to the others within the area or neighborhood, and the ROI (return of investment). This type of company also focuses more on selling such properties and taking advantage of networking as well as business and personal relationships when it comes to generating rapid sales for the clients.

- Property Management – Some companies are more involved in property management. This means managing the rental properties of owners or clients. Such clients encompass sole owners of one rental home who do not want to get involved in the daily issues often faced by landlords or landladies, or groups owning a few homes or apartment buildings.

  These owners may ask for help to manage their properties. Brokers here require expertise in tenant/landlord law. These brokers are responsible for maintaining the property and vetting renters, handling paperwork and payments for rentals, and securing tenants.

See? You have numerous options on the companies or firms where you can work at the start of your career. Take the time to research them. Learn the pros and cons of each company and apply them to your situation and skills. That way, you can Drake a better decision when choosing which one can stabilize your career and make you more recognizable in the industry.

Formulating Your Agency Shortlist

With the numerous options available for newbie real estate agents in terms of the companies to work for, you may get confused in the whole selection process. You don't have to rush. Take your time during the selection process, so you can choose one that fits you the best. As much as possible, try to land a job in a company that offers flexibility, especially in commission structure.

Also, look for a company capable of supporting your career growth, providing the guidance and training needed for your success, and shortening the learning curve for you. To formulate your agency shortlist more effectively and increase your chances of finding a stable company that is indeed right for you and your ideas, here are some key factors and pointers to consider:

Commission Split

A lot of real estate agents who are still starting their careers in the industry choose a company or brokerage firm based solely on commission splits. It is an important factor, really, but remember that it should never be your only deciding point. As a matter of fact, basing your decision only on the commission is a horrible way of selecting a company or broker to work for as a beginner.

Develop the mindset of giving the company a fair share or cut of the commission if they can actually contribute a lot in making your business fly, even if you are just a starter. The traditional brokerage model is paying the agent slightly over half of the earned commission. If this is the model that a specific company is working on, then you can also expect them to be the ones shouldering the overhead expenses.

You can also find brokers who are willing to provide you your full commission, meaning 100%, but you have to be more cautious if they offer you this payment scheme. The reason is that this approach may also mean that you will be paying them in other ways, like in the form of desk and transaction fees and E and O premiums. The worst part is if they don't actually provide you with any assistance.

With that said, a lot of agents say that it would be better to start with a smaller cut from the commission when they receive most, if not all, of the things they need from the company, including proper assistance and training. The good news is that as soon as your sales volume increases within the calendar year, you can also expect the percentage of your commission split to increase.

Company Culture

Make a shortlist of the best possible companies to work for based on company culture. For instance, an office filled mainly with new real estate agents may look full of energy, but it could also be chaotic every now and then.

If the company has mostly seasoned and experienced agents, it may have more stability than others. The problem is that it may also be lacking in terms of fun and excitement as well as in new-agent peer support.

If possible, look for a company that has a combination of both new and experienced agents, allowing you to enjoy the individual advantages of both cultures. After your interview with a potential broker or manager, take time to reflect and ask yourself about your actual feelings, not only about the person interviewing you but the company as a whole. Listen to your intuition and gut feelings, as this matters a lot in your final decision.

It would also be helpful for you to check out the website of the company, locate their directory, and contact a few agents who are already working there. Ask about their thoughts about the company as a workplace for both experienced and newbie agents. This will give you a feel of their actual culture and environment.

Size of the Office

If you are in a metropolitan area, your options may range from firms with only 10 agents or less to bigger companies employing hundreds of real estate agents. Larger firms most likely own more than just one office, so it would be better for you to consider the actual size of the office instead of the entire company.

Your personal preference matters a lot here. You may be someone who is more thrilled and motivated with the buzz and excitement that a large office demonstrates, or you could be someone who prefers a smaller office because you feel more comfortable with its provided cohesiveness. Reflect on which one between your options will let you maximize your full potential.

Location

The exact location of the company should also contribute to your final decision. Think about the length of time it usually takes for you to commute to and from your potential office. Yes, the newest technology nowadays provides agents like you with superior mobility, which means that it may be unnecessary to do all your work in the office.

However, there are still instances when you have to visit the office physically. It could be to check postal mails and attend meetings. It could also be that you are that type who prefers working in the office, instead of at home, since you feel like your productivity will be at an all-time high there.

With that in mind, you really have to think about the location. It does not necessarily need to be close to your home, but it should be easily accessible at the very least. Also, it will be up to you if you prefer your office to be in a shopping center, high-rise tower, or in a freestanding building.

The ultimate deciding factor in terms of location, though, should always be ease of access not only for you but also for your clients. They should be able to locate your office easily. The location should also allow consistent after-hours access.

Regular Employee vs. Independent Contractor

Another key factor when shortlisting various companies to work for is to find out what type of position you will be getting. Will it be as a regular employee or an independent contractor? Note that as a real estate agent, you can get affiliated with a brokerage firm or company as an independent contractor or a regular employee – both of which have their individual pros and cons.

If you are offered a spot in the company as a regular employee, then an incredible benefit you will enjoy will be a fixed salary on a regular basis. It also lets you share the social security/Medicare tax burden with your employer. You can also enjoy other rewarding benefits only available for regular employees, like health insurance, retirement funds, and stock options.

The problem is that all these perks provided by your employer also mean that they will be the ones with direct control over when, how, and where you execute your professional duties and responsibilities.

You may also be offered a position as an independent contractor. Based on the National Association of Realtors, around 90% of licensed real estate agents actually work as independent contractors. The reason behind this is that more and more brokerage firms prefer hiring these independent contractors due to simpler tax requirements and compensation. This approach also allows them to save money as far as employee benefits are concerned.

If you work as an independent contractor, then expect to be fully responsible for your income taxes. You will also not receive benefits from your employer. The good news is that it lets you claim business deductions that are not available for regular employees. You will also enjoy superior flexibility, especially when it comes to the where and the when parts of performing your professional duties.

For instance, while it is a requirement for regular employees to do floor duty, you will have a say about whether you will be doing this or not if you get hired as an independent contractor. However, take note that even if you have this flexibility, this role does not mean that you are your own boss. Your broker will still have direct involvement in your actions.

Online Presence

Of course, you will want to make sure that you will be working with a company that already has a strong presence online. It is a very crucial factor these days as everyone already uses the internet.

Every time you introduce yourself to someone and tell them that you are working for a specific brokerage firm, expect them to cross-reference you on your company's official website. With that said, find a company that has an attractive, professional-looking, and presentable website, plenty of positive reviews online, and which is consistent activity on social media.

Also, assess how the website presents each agent. Are they introduced and presented well? Does it allow the agents to link their own websites? The reason is that as a real estate agent, you also need to build your own site – one that is separate and not dependent on your chosen broker or company.

You need to have your own because that will let you build your brand. You should be able to link it without hassle to the company's website. That way, the company can fulfill its job of promoting not only its brand but also its agents.

Reputation

Regardless of whether you are living in the city or a small rural town with slim competition, it is necessary to consider the company's or broker's reputation before finally deciding to work for them. Avoid those that have already earned a bad reputation in the market. Find out which one among the many brokerage firms and companies in your area holds a solid track record of being good to their clients.

Determine if they are the go-to firms for those who are planning to buy and sell properties. Also, determine if their good reputation is in the residential or commercial field. The goal here is to work for a reputable firm or company with a position in the market that strongly reflects what you want to achieve specifically in this industry.

Level of Support

Select a brokerage firm depending on the amount and level of support you will be getting from them. Remember that as a beginner, you will need all the support and guidance you can get. In that case, determine the company's actual stance on education.

Are they capable of providing adequate educational courses and technology tools that you can use to start your career correctly? How about other relevant items, like marketing materials, signage, and business cards? Are they going to be provided?

Find out if the broker will also be available to talk to you about your deals. Can you easily ask for their advice regarding sales, negotiation, and marketing? Are there seasoned agents around who can offer valuable tips and advice while you are still starting?

All these are vital questions that you need to find answers to before choosing a company to work for. You need as much support and guidance as possible as you would never want to begin your first few years in the industry alone and unsure of what to do.

Market Visibility

Another key consideration is how visible the brokerage firm is in the market. Has it been in the industry for quite a while now? If that is the case, then how visible is it in the market? Are there visible signs about the company around the neighborhood and town? Does the local market have excellent name recognition for them? Finding answers to such questions as those can help you identify the level of popularity of a certain brokerage firm.

If the one you are looking at has been in the industry for several years already, then it is highly likely that they have already earned an excellent reputation around the town. It also helps to ask around about the company just so you will know its status in the area. It can help in assessing whether you also have a chance of attaining a reasonable level of success if you work for this company.

Determine the market share of the company, too. Do they have a good percentage of all the homes and properties sold in your area? What are their available marketing initiatives? Are all those helpful for agents who are trying to get leads? All the information you will gather based on those questions will surely direct you to the right company.

Hopefully, all the tips mentioned in this chapter will help you to select the right company to work for. The ultimate goal is to find a firm that can bring out the best in you and guide you toward attaining the professional growth you are aiming for.

Chapter 2

Digital Marketing Strategies for Real Estate Agents

Once you have landed a position in the specific real estate company of your choice, the next step is to polish up your marketing skills. Of course, being a real estate agent means that you have to work doubly hard to close deals as it is the key for you to survive in the industry and get your name recognized. In that case, you should tap into the digital marketing space as it is what most real estate agents and professionals use.

While you can still take advantage of traditional marketing, like newspapers and radio advertising, you no longer have to completely rely on those campaigns and materials to succeed. You can now take advantage of the digital and online world, which is actually good, as millions of people are now using it. Going digital in all your marketing and promotional campaigns can benefit you in several ways – among which are:

- Saves time – The reason is that digital marketing allows you to reach your target audience quickly while promoting your brand in less time. With that, you will have more time on your hands to show properties instead of wasting it searching for leads.

- Provides access to qualified prospects – It lets you take advantage of inbound marketing tools to attract qualified leads instead of looking for them on your own. It can significantly increase the rate of conversion organically since prospective clients tend to reach out actively when searching for the perfect real estate company for them.

- Gives you exposure – Digital marketing can also help to expand your reach and give you your desired exposure to your target audience. The bigger the targeted audience you can attract, the bigger the potential of closing deals.

- Promotes ease in evaluating performance – Another great thing about digital marketing is that you can easily track the performance and results of the specific techniques you are using. You can even measure the returns and results of your efforts and their level of effectiveness when finding the perfect match in terms of clients.

- Promotes superior client engagement – Digital marketing can add more value to your brand, which can also equate to earning the trust and loyalty of your target clients. This gives you the chance to build long-term client relationships, securing you as the top choice anytime they search for property investments.

Digital marketing has indeed made a mark in the real estate industry. It is broad and extensive, which means that it provides real estate agents with plenty of tactics and strategies they can use to compensate their marketing efforts. Using that, you can tap into various digital marketing channels guaranteed to make you profitable and successful even if you are still a beginner.

YouTube Marketing

YouTube marketing is one of the most effective and powerful digital marketing strategies that work for real estate agents. This digital marketing technique requires you to post engaging videos to grab the attention of your target audience. What's great about using videos is that they can add more personality and dimension to your brand as well as your visual listings. Most people also tend to get easily hooked when viewing interesting video content.

Creating videos and posting them on YouTube can contribute to building your online reputation. It can help increase the number of leads and your rankings on search engines. You can create YouTube videos to share your professional perspectives about the industry, which can lead to a sudden surge of inquiries and successful deals. But the question is, why use YouTube when there are also other video-sharing websites?

Owned by Google, YouTube holds the second spot in the top-ranking search engines worldwide. This means it has an extensive and broad reach, which is good if you want to reach millions of users. You can also fully trust its reliability as far as streaming video content is concerned. This is vital, especially in today's market, where most people only have short attention spans.

Apart from that, YouTube assures users of seamless integration and support in Google's search results. The reason is that Google is fully aware of the usual challenges and difficulties in creating high-quality videos. Because of that, expect Google to weigh video contents differently every time they compute webpage rankings. This results in them seamlessly integrating and supporting videos in search results.

However, just like other forms of marketing, you need to know exactly how to use YouTube to your best advantage. Look for ways to ensure that your YouTube marketing efforts will result in better engagement. Your goal is to use your videos to make yourself recognizable in the industry, thereby increasing your chance of establishing relationships with potential clients. You can achieve that through these YouTube marketing tips:

Create a YouTube Channel and Optimize It

Undoubtedly, YouTube has several competitors in the online video marketing scene. However, despite such fierce competition, it is still a superior platform for real estate agents who would like to try video marketing considering its huge number of users – around a billion users in different parts of the world.

Note, though, that you can't reach this specific number of viewers effortlessly. You still need to create video content with a targeted niche and audience. You also have to work on optimizing your YouTube channel. Through proper optimization, you can target the specific users you are planning to reach.

Ensure That Your Channel Page Looks Appealing

Speaking of optimizing your YouTube channel, one way to achieve that is to make your channel page as appealing as possible. It should be as attractive as your official website and that of the company you belong to. Remember that you need to reinforce your brand's visual aspects anywhere you plan to build your online presence, including your YouTube channel.

A great way to improve the look of your channel is to put a profile image and banner at the top of your homepage. It also needs to have your headshot, contact info, and company name. Also, integrate an attractive and stylish image of one of your most impressive listings. All these features in your channel can make it more appealing, which can entice prospects to view your posted videos and contact you easily.

Also, add company details in your channel's "about" section. Avoid assuming that your target audience is already aware of how to access your site or communicate with you on social media. You have to let them know how they can reach out to you. You can do that by including links in your "about" section, so your target audience can easily find you in the digital universe. They should be able to contact you via phone or email, so add such details in that section, too.

Create Appealing Titles/Headlines for Your Videos

Think of captivating headlines or titles for your YouTube videos that your target viewers can easily find while inspiring more clicks. It is similar to when you create witty, attractive, and SEO-friendly titles for your real estate blogs. The headlines also need to come with relevant keywords and entice potential viewers to take a look at your clips.

To help you, visit the AdWords keyword planner of Google to figure out the most applicable and appropriate terms for your videos. Your chosen keywords and terms also need to be suitable for your overall marketing approach. Apart from AdWords' keyword planner, you may use other reliable keyword research tools at present.

Once you have gathered the appropriate keywords, organize them in such a way that you can spread them across all your videos. If you are using multiple keywords, then integrate them into the headline in such a way that they can maximize and expand your reach. Spend time reviewing the results of using these keywords, too. Find out which among the integrated phrases and words generated the highest number of clicks.

Upon taking hold of a list of keywords that seem to provide you with the best results, start using your imagination and creativity, so you can craft the best titles for every video content you have. Formulate various choices for the titles of each clip and pick one, which does not only sound natural when you read it but is also unique when you compare it to the other similar videos on YouTube.

Search for YouTube videos with content quite similar to yours. Check the headlines that have already been used, so you can avoid using them again. Your goal here is to make your title unique from the others while still generating interest from your target viewers. If you are thinking of posting a series of YouTube videos, then create a recurring title – one that allows you to use and incorporate subtitles every time you post a new episode.

Post Valuable Video Content

Your YouTube videos will play a significant and major role in grabbing the attention of prospective viewers. It is why you have to make each one truly relevant and interesting. Each video should be interesting and engaging enough that it will inspire your viewers to return to your channel to watch more of your videos and learn more about you.

Have a long-term vision of the specific goals you want your channel to achieve. This vision is what will guide you in crafting your content. Also, practice consistency in terms of the production, graphics, value proposition, and video length. Identify the specific angles and the subject matter guaranteed to inform your target audience. You should then prioritize and hone the details of every video based on them.

You may also want to check out the following options for video content that your target audience will find relevant:

- How-to – This type encompasses explanatory clips on the usual tasks that all sellers and buyers of properties have to accomplish. Some valuable topics for this video content include how to set an asking price and how to secure a home loan. What's great about posting how-to videos is that they can give you the chance to position yourself as an expert capable of providing useful information to your viewers.

- Interviews – You can also do interviews for your YouTube videos. You may want to interview those who have interesting knowledge, backgrounds, and stories in the industry, including business owners and restaurateurs in your locality. They are the best people to interview on camera, so you can emphasize the local market where the properties you are promoting are located.

- Market updates – Another great idea for your YouTube video marketing campaign would be market updates. You may want to feed your target viewers with information about the recent updates in the real estate market. Note that both sellers and buyers want to gather information about whether or not the market has a potential for growth in certain areas, such as employment opportunities and home values. Cover that in your channel, and you will surely attract new leads.

- Listings – This type is perhaps the most popular format used by real estate agents when integrating videos into their marketing campaigns. What you should do is display your listings in your videos. Do it in such a way that they can leave a great impression on your viewers. Your ultimate goal should be to entice them to check out your listings.

- Neighborhood overviews – These videos are not as popular as listings, but you can expect them to give you an idea about what it would feel like to live in the market or neighborhood you are focusing on. Make sure you highlight the best qualities of the community in these videos, so you can capture the interest of your audience.

When producing YouTube videos regarding real estate, avoid reinventing the wheel too much. What you should do, instead, is determine the specific things that helped other agents attain success in their video marketing campaigns. After that, identify a distinctive means of spinning and adding your unique version to such clips so that they become suitable for your channel.

For example, if you find a video featuring what it feels like to be in the market that an agent is focusing on, including restaurants, neighborhoods, and businesses there, then you can also follow the same format when creating your own content.

Just make sure that you write your own script. Add your own flair to your video, too. Apart from that, ensure that there are long-tail keywords relevant to real estate in the tags, descriptions, and the titles of your videos. By doing that, sellers and buyers in your specific market can easily find and discover them.

Post Videos Frequently

More frequent posting of relevant and valuable YouTube videos is also the key to attaining success in this campaign. If you post engaging videos relevant to real estate regularly, then you can continue connecting with your viewers.

If possible, produce at least one video that you can post every week. This frequency is usually enough to garner more interest from your target audience and make them want to subscribe to your channel. It also increases your chances of getting shortlisted by anyone who plans to sell or buy a property. It is possible if YouTube users become more familiar with you and what you offer.

Are you planning to post more than one video every week? Then make sure you develop themes as this can help inform your target viewers of what to expect from your channel. For instance, you can set a day for a particular theme (ex. Mondays – for tips and tricks, Wednesdays – for videos that inform buyers about the positive benefits of dealing with a real estate agent, etc.). Just give your viewers an idea of what to look forward to on a certain day.

Add Thumbnails and Optimize Them

Thumbnails are also vital components for your YouTube video marketing campaigns as they play a major role in search optimization. The thumbnail image is what a lot of users will see whenever they search for a YouTube video in your niche. It will appear in their search together with your video's title and the start of its description.

You don't have to take this thumbnail from a frame in your video, but it should be capable of relaying every clip's focal point. The most effective thumbnails are usually those that are:

- At least 640x360 pixels

- Visually compelling

- Accurate representations of your content

Avoid using irrelevant or pixelated images. It should not lack of cohesiveness either. Otherwise, they can result in poor click rates. It may also lead to problems in your overall branding efforts. Remember that most of your target viewers crave consistency and quality content, so try to show that in every significant element and component of your video marketing campaign. It is the key to capturing their interest.

Best Practices to Implement in Your YouTube Channel

Now that you are aware of some tips that you can use for your YouTube video marketing campaign, it is time for you to start producing your videos. When filming and editing your real estate videos, be reminded of the following best practices:

- Keep the videos short but engaging and informative – Note that shorter videos tend to obtain a higher rate of engagement, so shorten your content as much as possible. Around 2 to 5 minutes of content is usually enough.

- Use a notecard or script every time you speak in front of the camera – It can contribute to delivering a more concise and clearer message.

- Integrate a call to action in every posted video – An example would be encouraging your prospective clients to fill out the form incorporated in the page. That way, you can easily reach out to them or share valuable information.

- Share your videos on social media and online pages – This means including a link to your YouTube videos in your social media accounts, like Facebook, incorporating them in your newsletters, and adding them to your website.

The most challenging part of creating real estate videos for your YouTube marketing campaign is determining how to start. But just like other things, once you get the hang of it and learn the ins and outs of video marketing, you will reap great rewards, such as an improved reputation in the industry and a better online presence. All these can help you to gain clients and close deals.

Facebook Marketing

Facebook is also another platform in the digital marketing space that you should consider tapping into. Many agents, whether newbie and experienced, favor this platform for targeting social media users. With around two billion active users worldwide, Facebook is indeed an expansive space to tap into. It allows you to reach a wide range of potential clients.

Facebook marketing also seems to provide numerous favorable advantages to both seasoned and newbie agents – among which are the following:

- Cost-effective – It is cost-effective as it allows you to advertise and promote your brand while spending less - even as little as just $5. Using traditional marketing strategies requires you to spend a lot more to reach the same number of clients.

- Targeted promotions and advertising – Facebook marketing lets you promote and market your services to a certain group. It leads to a more targeted approach in advertising as you can direct it to people depending on their specific age, location, interest, and behavior.

- Builds brand awareness – With its millions of users, you will get the chance to make your brand more recognizable through Facebook. The good news is that as your audience gets more familiar with you and your skills, you can also increase the chances of them dealing with you.

- Provides measurable results – This means that you can measure your progress and check if your marketing campaigns are working. It provides measurable results in the sense that you can conveniently see the number of clicks, conversions, and impressions you are receiving.

- Encourages more engagement with your audience – Engagement, in this case, refers to the likes, interactions, and comments received by your Facebook ads. It shows the level of engagement and connection you have established with your target audience. If you keep on engaging them, then you will also have a higher chance of converting them into actual paying clients. The good engagement you can acquire through Facebook can even result in referrals, especially if people start sharing your real estate posts.

- Allows remarketing – Remarketing refers to an advertising strategy that makes it possible for you to advertise to website visitors who have recently viewed your ad. It allows you to retarget even those visitors who do not take action. What's even more amazing about this remarketing strategy is that it can also significantly raise your conversions while improving your career and reputation as a real estate agent.

- Allows you to feature listings – You can add video tours, pictures, and information about your listings, making your page as engaging as possible to your target audience. Remember that good quality walk-through videos help potential clients to see the properties you are marketing.

In addition, Facebook also gives you the opportunity to share your accomplishments in the industry. This is actually a big thing for beginners like you who are still going through the stages of making a name for themselves. You just have to inform your Facebook page followers of your successes.

You can even post about the houses you have successfully sold, so you can let your followers know that you already have several happy and satisfied clients who continue to trust you. Now, the question is, how can you achieve all the above-mentioned benefits? If you want to take full advantage of the power of Facebook marketing, then you may want to implement these tips in your campaigns:

Create a Facebook Page

Avoid using your personal account on Facebook for business. It is important to create your own page – one that is specifically meant for business. Setting up your own Facebook page, which is mainly designed for your real estate brand, is the first step toward using this social network for marketing.

The good thing about having your business page set up is that it gives you access to tools, analytics, and features not accessible and available when you are using your personal account. Having your Facebook page can strengthen your online presence, which can contribute a lot to attaining long-term success. Apart from that, a Facebook page looks more professional, so expect to be able to market to your target audience and followers more efficiently.

With a Facebook page, you also get the chance to gather up to several million followers, a feature not available in a personal account as it limits the number of friends to 5,000. However, remember that this process does not end in just setting it up. You also need to work on your page in order to make it effective in attracting your target audience and generating leads.

In that case, boost the effectiveness of your page through the following:

- Uploading a professional-looking profile picture – Keep in mind that your logo or headshot is often the first component of your page that people see every time they visit it. It is the reason why you have to choose a professional and vibrant one. Pick a profile photo for your Facebook page that is the appropriate size, specifically using 180x180 pixels or 360x360 pixel format.

- Updating your cover photo – You also need to use the most appropriate and engaging cover photo you can find, as it can help to leave a good first impression on your audience. The cover photo for your Facebook page can be an image containing graphics or a video. A great example would be a picture of properties you have successfully offered to your clients. For your cover photo, the suggested size is around 820x360 pixels.

- Including your contact details – Do not forget to include information about how your Facebook page visitors can contact you. In most cases, these visitors will want to gather information on how to reach out to you, especially if they are serious about doing business with a real estate agent.

- To make your page look more professional and legitimate, include your office address, email address, phone number, and website URL. Add your business hours or the specific times of the day when you will be accepting inquiries.

- Incorporating a call to action (CTA) – What is great about Facebook is that it allows the integration of a large call to action to your page. It comes in the form of a huge blue button, which is an incredible feature as it helps you to capture more leads. It lets you generate more traffic to a certain link or direct people to the messaging inbox so they can send inquiries.

You can also choose from the various CTAs provided by Facebook, including "Download," "Send Message," "Contact Us," "Learn More," and "Apply Now." Just pick one you think is compelling enough for those who see your ads or visit your Facebook business page. Another advantage is you can customize the CTAs in accordance with your wants and preferences.

For instance, you can integrate this CTA, "Check Out My Profile," in your cover image if you have a real estate profile on another site. By encouraging your audience to take action, you will be able to attract new leads who are qualified enough and have a high chance of wanting to do business with you. Make sure that your call to action is engaging and compelling enough, so you can achieve that purpose.

Use or Join a Facebook Group

You can also make the most out of Facebook marketing by using or joining a group. A Facebook group is different from your business page. It acts as a place on Facebook where people who have similar interests gather together as a means of discussing topic/s of interest. Perhaps real estate in your geographical location is the focus of this group.

An advantage of joining or creating a group on Facebook that tackles real estate is that it promotes better focus compared to the free-wheeling discussions usually happening in one's newsfeed. Also, it is different from your page in the sense that the Facebook group prioritizes interacting with the members instead of focusing on your brand and business.

Another advantage of being part of a Facebook group is that it prioritizes conversations. It also allows you to establish a relationship with your prospects and clients and widen your reach. It is even an opportunity to select whatever it is that you want the group to focus on, especially if you are the one who started it.

For instance, you can start a Facebook group with the main focus on selling and buying properties in the specific state or neighborhood you are working in. It helps you attract people who are seriously thinking about buying or selling a home in your area or neighborhood. In this group, the members can talk to each other and with you regarding their journey toward selling or buying property in your area.

If people focus on things that they genuinely find interesting, establishing good relationships will be a lot easier. For real estate agents like you, the process of building a relationship is an important yet challenging job. You can make this process easier and simpler with a Facebook group. The members will even start looking at you as an agent. It also helps awaken their interest in your brand.

The members of the group even have the chance to connect with you personally. Moreover, the group you create may be an excellent means of fostering evangelists for your real estate brand. This will most likely happen during or after a successful sale or purchase of a property.

Another thing that Facebook groups can do is allow you to post content with more organic reach compared to pages. This is a good thing as organic reach is known to cost significantly less compared to active advertising.

Take Advantage of Facebook Ads

Facebook marketing is not just about setting up a successful page and then waiting for it to do something for you. Yes, it is important, but it is not the only thing that will contribute to acquiring tons of high-quality and targeted leads for your business.

Remember that lead generation on Facebook does not only involve post boosting, name recognition, or acquiring engagements or likes. Referrals are also helpful from members whose friends are looking for property. You can make your page even more effective when it comes to generating leads by using it as an inbound marketing channel capable of driving people to your site instead of just to your posts on Facebook.

Avoid making the mistake of other agents who are more caught up with the number of fans or friends they have or the number of comments and likes received by their posts. Make yourself different by using your Facebook page as a tool for inbound marketing, which can contribute a lot to them clicking on your site. These clicks are actually more important than likes, shares, and comments.

A great way to acquire such high-quality leads is to begin running targeted ads through this popular social network's ad program. The good news is that Facebook provides various advertising options that you can manipulate to attain various goals. Because of that, you can use its ad program to zone in on prospective clients, drive website traffic, and create more awareness about being a real estate agent. Use the upgraded and advanced tools in the Facebook advertising program to create ads that target the specific kinds of people who intend to buy or sell a house or property within the next six months.

You can also take advantage of the lead generation ability of Facebook ads by specifically targeting an audience with major life-changing situations. By using this feature, you can target those who just got engaged, married, or gave birth. Remember that new parents and newlyweds are the ones who are often interested in buying new homes or properties, so they are the perfect people to target when you are planning to use Facebook ads.

Another advantage of using the advertising program on Facebook is that it provides a distinctive way of targeting people depending on their most current behaviors. This strategy for advanced demographic targeting is useful when advertising to specific people with a much better chance of them needing the services of a real estate agent. The good news is that you can use this specific feature at a low price, less than just $5 daily.

Apart from all the advantages mentioned, you can also use the programs Ads Manager app. It is useful to manage every ad that you have posted and track their individual performance. You can keep track of the number of people who have seen your ad and the actions they took after seeing it. The app is also valuable as it lets you do several things, like fixing typos seamlessly, changing pictures, scheduling your ads, making adjustments to your budget, and editing your chosen audience.

It even notifies you whenever you have an ad that is about to end. It also sends a notification once you are about to reach your spending limit. Once you get notified of that, you can easily make some changes to your payment methods and set up your new spending limit. It will also give you an idea about the amount you spent on your previous ad campaigns.

Additional Tips for Facebook Marketing

Apart from the already mentioned guidelines, you can use Facebook marketing to your best advantage by following these simple tips:

- Set up the chat feature – You need the chat feature/function of Facebook, so you can quickly respond to inquiries or anything that your target audience may want to discuss regarding your business. Remember that the majority of active social media users nowadays will want to receive a response in less than an hour or within the day whenever they send a message to a company. You can meet that expectation by activating Facebook's chat feature. You can even take advantage of its saved replies and automated responses.

- Allow reviews – Make sure that your Facebook page allows your followers and clients to post reviews. These reviews can help build your reputation. Almost all shoppers want to read reviews online before spending their money on something, and this also includes purchases derived from legitimate providers of those services.

- Show off good reviews to boost your prospective client's confidence in doing business with you. You may also want to moderate or turn off certain reviews. Every time you have successfully closed a deal, thank your clients, then provide them with the link to your page on Facebook so they can leave a review.

- Have a detailed target audience – Whenever you create your ad campaign on Facebook, it is necessary to decide on a detailed target audience. You need to define your target audience, the ones who will most likely engage with you, as this can increase the chances of your ads succeeding. You can make your target audience more detailed by choosing the age, location, interest, country, and radius, among many other factors that you would like to target.

- Add helpful tabs – Ensure that your Facebook page has tabs that your followers will find useful. Incorporate a tab capable of highlighting the listings that you feature. That way, your audience will be able to click on any listing that captures their interest.

- Do not ignore comments on your page – Respond to both bad and good comments promptly. This is a wise move and will earn the respect and trust of your present and prospective clients since it indicates that you pay attention to them.

- Post videos and photos on your Facebook page – It would be best to add some pictures and videos every time you post something on your page. The reason is that these posts result in better engagement. It is also a great way to interact with your audience.

- Stick to local interests – Most of your followers will be interested to know the things that are taking place in the local community. This is particularly true for anyone who just moved to a new and unfamiliar place. Your posts, therefore, should be regarding charity events in the locality and school-related events and activities. Emphasize a famous local business. Generally, your posts should be regarding anything that makes the community of your focus more interesting and appealing to your audience.

- Post pictures of you and your entire team as well as your happy and satisfied clients. Your Facebook page needs to have pictures of you and your team in maybe office parties or community functions. These images can provide a personal and actual face to your business. Note that your prospective clients are interested in finding out whether they are interacting with real and legitimate people, not corporations without a face.

Aside from your team's pictures, post images of your happy and satisfied clients, too, particularly as they stand next to the home they have just bought. These pictures prove that you are indeed someone that people can trust when they need the help of a real estate agent.

The most important tip in Facebook marketing, though, is to be extra patient. Note that you can't expect to grow your business and generate leads and sales through Facebook overnight. It may take time, effort, and sometimes, money, so you need to be really patient. Everything will be worth it in the end, though, especially as you notice your brand gaining more and more exposure and the number of your followers significantly increasing.

Instagram Marketing

Another highly effective and powerful digital marketing strategy that you can use is by tapping into social media is Instagram marketing. Instagram is one of those big-name platforms in social media that can help real estate agents increase the number of their potential leads significantly and improve their business. Through Instagram, you can show off your new properties and help those who are interested in doing business with you contact you with ease.

However, just like other digital marketing tactics and social media channels for marketing, you need to know the ins and outs of Instagram marketing to make the most of it. Here, you will learn some tips and tricks that will let you take full advantage of Instagram when it comes to capturing the attention of your target audience.

Create a Business Profile

Similar to Facebook marketing, it would be best for you to set up your own business account on Instagram instead of using your personal account. After all, you will be using it for business and marketing, so it would be in your best interest to separate your personal account from your business account. One great advantage of having your real estate business set up on Instagram is that it provides easy and immediate access to analytics. It allows you to view details, including the following, in an instant:

- Post interactions every week, including website clicks and profile visits
- Weekly page discovers, including the reach and impressions of your posts
- Number of posts you publish every week
- Audience demographics
- Post-performance, which can be measured based on the number of views each post receives

All these details will be useful to monitor each of your post's engagement and impressions. Another reason to create your own business account is that it gives your prospective clients the chance to communicate with you easily. Just make sure you incorporate your contact details in your profile, like your phone number and email address.

That way, those who visit your Instagram page do not have to leave it just to get your contact details. This is a good thing as the easier your followers and target audience can contact and communicate with you, the higher the chances of you acquiring new leads. Having a professional business account on Instagram also means you can publish and create ads there without having to use the ad tools on Facebook.

Optimize Your Business Profile

To maximize your business profile, you have to optimize it. Optimizing your Instagram profile can help you become more visible in this digital space. One way to do it is to add an inviting and appealing bio. Think of it as the first thing that other real estate agents, as well as your target audience, will see and that can leave a good impression on them.

Think carefully about how to post your bio. A wise tip is to make it brief but inviting. It should also contain relevant details, like what you do, your specific niche, location, and call-to-action. As for the niche, indicate your focus, like commercial real estate, residential property, or beach-front.

Apart from your bio, you also need to integrate a professional profile picture. Choose a professional-looking one. It should be capable of showing how trustworthy and reliable you are, even for those who have not met you yet. Also, use the photo gallery in your Instagram account, so you can continue leaving a positive impression on your leads.

Another way to optimize your profile is to include a link to your blog or actual website along with your contact number. By doing that, anyone interested in doing business with you can visit your site to gather more information about the services you offer. It offers convenience when it comes to inviting people to take the next step once they visit your site, and that is contacting you for their real estate needs.

Look for Influencers Who Also Focus on Your Chosen Niche

One thing that you should remember about using Instagram for marketing and promotions is that influencers are now booming on this social media platform. With influencer marketing being popular nowadays, it will help a lot to partner with influencers within the same niche as yours.

This kind of partnership is good for your business as it allows you to make your services more visible to a bigger chunk of your target audience. For instance, if you successfully closed deals with some influencers, then do not forget to ask them to inform their followers about their experience upon getting in touch with you. You may also request that these influencers incorporate a link back to your Instagram account.

By partnering with influencers, you can tap into a larger market, considering the fact that they usually have several thousand to millions of followers. However, remember that when choosing an influencer to partner with, the exact number of followers is not as important as how engaged such followers are.

Find out if the followers of a particular influencer are truly engaged with them. You can assess the level of their engagements with the influencer if they leave comments, like posts, and share content. Also, determine whether the majority of the influencer's followers closely match your target clients.

Provided you use influencer marketing correctly, it can significantly raise your chance of building awareness about you as a real estate agent and get your services known to those seeking a real estate agent. This is a good thing, especially if you are still new in the industry or currently working independently.

Try to Learn From the Famous Influencers in Your Chosen Niche

Speaking of influencer marketing, it also helps to emulate what they do, especially when it comes to using Instagram. Educate yourself on how to use Instagram effectively by learning about the exact hashtags they usually use and their call to action. Learn from the captions they include in their posts, too.

For instance, if they usually post questions to followers, determine the level of engagement they receive from it. Study the types of content they often share, too, and assess the usual responses of their followers. By doing that, you will get an idea about what seems to work in terms of engaging followers. The goal here is not to copy them completely. You just have to find out the strategy that works for them and identify how you can make it better and more relevant to your business.

Incorporate Plenty of Useful and Relevant Hashtags in Your Posts

On Instagram, hashtags are extremely important as these can be of help when categorizing your posted content and making your target audience locate it easily. These hashtags refer to keywords that those who use Instagram can follow or search for. Hashtags are powerful when it comes to reaching out to your target audience, so make sure to use the correct ones.

Instagram actually allows you to use a max of 30 hashtags for every post, but it is highly advisable not to overdo it. Set limits to avoid making your posts look spammy. It would be best to just stick to around 10 to 12 hashtags and ensure that they are valuable and relevant to your posted content.

Another wise tip is to stick to hashtags that only contain 2-3 words as they are more targeted. By doing that, these targeted hashtags can surely drive more traffic not only to your Instagram page but also to your official website. It also helps to take a look at the hashtags used by other real estate agents in your niche. You can emulate them but make sure that such hashtags are proven to be popular.

Your hashtags also need to be as targeted and specific as possible. For instance, if your focus is selling houses and lots in Arizona, then you may want to use "arizonahouseandlotforsale" or arizonahouseandlot as your hashtags. The goal here is to use the most suitable and appropriate hashtags capable of driving pertinent traffic.

Post Stunning Pictures of Real Estate

Being a real estate agent may have made you realize that first impressions almost always last. It is true, especially when it comes to your real estate posts on Instagram. With that said, you have to make it a point to post stunning real estate images all the time. In that case, remind yourself of the importance of good lighting.

Invest in proper lighting equipment and a tripod whether you use a professional camera or your phone to capture pictures. Remember that poor lighting may only dissuade your target audience from checking out your posts. It may also affect the quality of the pictures. Your goal when capturing pictures is to make them look professional and stunning with the right lighting. You can achieve that with these simple tips:

- Buy a lens for your phone's camera – This is something that you should invest in if you plan on using your mobile phone for taking real estate pictures. The lens can contribute a lot to improving the quality of the images you capture.

- Invest in a professional camera – There is no better way to improve the quality of your pictures and make them as stunning as possible than to use a professional camera. Just make sure you research the different kinds of cameras you can use so you can pick one that fits your budget while promoting ease and convenience every time you need to take pictures.

- Use a similar filter for each photo – This can provide your Instagram with a more consistent feel and look. This consistency can make your page look more credible and trustworthy.

- Edit your photo to the perfect image size – If necessary, crop each picture, so it will be at the appropriate size of 1080x1350 or 4x4 aspect ratio. This means that every picture you post should be around 1350 pixels tall and 1080 wide. It is the perfect size as it allows the pictures to use the maximum vertical space every time users scroll through your Instagram feed.

- Seek the help of an expert – If you feel like you have no talent in taking great pictures, then seeking the help of an expert photographer can help. The good thing about working with an expert is that they can also assist in photo editing, handling lighting details, and providing you with valuable tips on framing the perfect shot.

However, if you intend to hire a third-party company, then make plans in advance since most of these professional photographers usually take a lot of time to edit and process pictures.

Again, your goal here is to make your Instagram page more attractive to your audience by ensuring that you fill it up with relevant and stunning images. Every picture and each piece of content you post also needs to be capable of speaking your brand. This is necessary to showcase the best in you as a real estate agent.

Look at your Instagram page as your business logo, business card, website, and brand font. It is one of the things that a lot of your target audience will see about you. It is also representative of you, your team, your brand, and your services.

With that in mind, you need to stay consistent when it comes to posting quality and appealing content and pictures. Ensure that the content and pictures showcase a sense of knowledge, experience, and trust, too.

Take Advantage of Targeted Ads

Targeted ads on Instagram have also become popular recently. Take advantage of them when it comes to putting your name out there and making yourself more recognizable. The good news is that you can set an ad budget, so you will have full control over the specific amount you intend to spend on each one. You can also choose to showcase a sponsored ad in the form of just one image or several images in one carousel.

Before you take advantage of sponsored posts, remember the only ones who can see your pictures are your followers. Once you have decided to make a sponsored ad, craft and use content that will keep users engaged.

The content also needs to appeal to your target demographic, the one who you intend the ad to reach. Do not forget to include a clear CTA (call-to-action), so the users who get to view your content and ad can easily contact or call you and visit your site.

Look for the Best Angle for Your Pictures

Every time you take pictures for Instagram marketing, look for a particular way to show off your listings impressively. An effective way to do that is to find the perfect angle for the pictures. You can achieve that through the following:

- Show the exteriors – Note that a lot of those who are part of your target audience want to have an idea of what a home's exterior looks like, so focus on that. The home's interior often comes as second. As a matter of fact, it is okay for you to just add the details regarding the interiors later, once you have already written the caption. Capture the interest of your prospective clients by demonstrating to them what and how it feels like to own a property from your listings. Help them to see the curb appeal.

- Utilize the carousel or collage feature – Instagram has a carousel or collage feature that you can use to highlight more than just one fantastic feature of your listing. It is a photo editing feature, which lets you post several pictures in just one post. With that, you get the chance to show off all the impressive features of your listings instead of only one.

- Share floor plans – Do you wish to focus on selling new housing developments or pre-builds? Then the best way to showcase them in your Instagram feed is to share floor plans. You may want to display layouts and floor plans to prospective buyers occasionally, particularly to those who want to get the first scoop when a property becomes available to the market.

Your ultimate goal here is to highlight the best out of your listings through your posted pictures on Instagram. That way, you can encourage users to talk to you and do business with you.

Add Videos to Your Feed

Instagram is not only meant to show pictures. You can also use it to show the videos you have captured regarding your listings. Note that in just a couple of years, online videos have started to dominate consumer internet traffic. Avoid getting left behind by beginning to record a few videos of your listings now.

Aside from being an extremely vital component of every marketing plan, social media posts containing videos can be expected to have a higher number of views compared to just static pictures. The good thing about garnering more views for your listings is that they can also capture the interest of prospective buyers.

If you are still a beginner in this approach, then an effective strategy that you can work on is to capture a short video that walks through every listing. Another tip is to integrate live 360 videos in your IGTV or Instagram story. To entice your followers to watch your live update, create a recap then post it in your Instagram feed.

Feature Restaurants, Business, and Local Attractions

You can also entice your target clients by posting pictures of what is around the property you are offering to the public. For instance, you may want to post pictures of attractions and restaurants within the locality. By doing that, you can make your listings look more attractive. With these pictures, you get the chance to provide your prospects with a glimpse around the neighborhood.

Aside from pictures, you may also want to take a short video that shows off the neighborhood. Capture videos and images of community parties and retreats, too. Make sure that your prospective clients look at the images and view the videos every time so that they will be inspired to think about moving to that location.

Feature Your Clients

Your Instagram should not only be filled with pictures and videos relevant to your listings. You may also want to use it to show off your successful business dealings with clients. Every time you close a deal or hand over a key to a new homeowner, ask their permission to capture the moment on camera.

Take an image to celebrate that day. Just remember that the moment you will be capturing is about them, not you, so ask for their permission before posting them on Instagram. Give them the freedom to choose how they want to pose for the picture, too.

Google SEO

Google SEO is also another of the most convenient yet cost-effective digital marketing strategies for real estate agents. It can build up your brand identity, increase the number of your leads and actual clients, and boost your profit. By incorporating Google SEO in your digital marketing campaigns, you can easily keep in touch with your present clients and reach out to more leads and prospects.

Through Google search engine optimization (SEO), you also get the chance to boost your visibility online. You will get your services discovered by local people, which can contribute a lot to boosting the results of your digital marketing campaign despite the tough competition in the industry.

Another great thing about local SEO is that it helps you rank higher on Google, which is what can make your business more recognizable and visible. It can capture the interest of prospective buyers and help you survive any kind of crisis, even a pandemic. To take full advantage of Google SEO, implement these tips:

Use Tools for SEO Analysis

Before you even begin your journey toward marketing through effective SEO, you should do a better analysis of the present situation. The good thing about using these tools is that they can be extremely valuable to measure the quality of your website as far as optimization is concerned.

The first thing that Google Analytics can do for you is to identify the specific pages on your website that need maximum optimization. You may want to use the "Search Console" of Google to detect SEO issues requiring your immediate attention.

To ensure that your content optimization efforts will not be put to waste, use the most effective tools for it, including Grammarly, Yoast, and SEO Surfer. These are paid sites, but setting a budget for them every month can benefit you a lot.

If possible, use the tools' premium versions as they tend to deliver much better performance.

Also, make sure that you are capable of tracking backlinks, so you can maintain the high engagement rate of your website. You can actually use several tools to track backlinks and determine the spam score and domain authority of your site. Among the best examples are Moz and Ahrefs. The good news is that these two sites feature Chrome extensions that are extremely helpful if you want to have an easier time accomplishing some tasks.

Perform an SEO Audit Beforehand

An SEO audit is a huge help in identifying the specific pages that deliver incredible performance as well as the specific areas that you need to improve. While this process is kind of time-consuming, you will find it valuable as it acts as your benchmark when measuring your progress. You can use it to gather the information necessary to create or build a roadmap. It helps you answer the following relevant questions:

• Is your website ranking well locally?

• Are you gaining organic traffic?

• Are you successful when it comes to generating and converting leads?

If you have negative responses to these questions, then be aware that there are specific reasons for such problems, and you can perform the SEO audit to identify them. When doing the audit, focus on key areas, including:

- Your website structure, including redirects, robots.txt, and XML sitemap.

- Your page structure, including titles, heading tags, URLs, alt tags, and meta description.

- Content, including link and keyword placement, structure, redirects, canonical tags, duplicates, and visual elements.

- Links, including inbound and outbound links, broken links, and interlinks with other site's pages.

- Usability, including site speed, mobile-friendliness, and accessibility.

Improve the mentioned key areas to optimize your site for a better Google search engine ranking. This can help improve organic traffic. In this case, you may want to take advantage of Google analytics, so you will get an idea about the specific pages that require immediate attention.

You may also want to use the Search Console of Google to detect issues requiring fixing. Other tools you have to use during the SEO audit are the PageSpeed Insights tool and the Mobile-friendly test feature.

Claim Your My Business Listing on Google

This is a vital step in local search engine optimization as it allows you to list all the details regarding your business in Google – among which are your business name, phone number, and address. Use consistent details, especially name, address, and contact number, across all your digital platforms and channels, like your social media accounts and pages and your official website.

Upon claiming your My Business listing, expect to begin showing up on the knowledge cards on Google Maps, SERPs, and 3 Pack. You should also let your My Business Listing in Google get verified. Once that happens, you get the chance to make citation accounts in many other online channels and places, like Facebook, Foursquare, Yellow Pages, and Yelp.

This means that any user who looks for real estate listings or agencies on other platforms, not just Google, will be able to find you in the results. This can boost your visibility, which is a major contributor when trying to generate leads.

Conduct Extensive Keyword Research Appropriate for the Real Estate Industry

Analyze various real estate keywords so you know which ones are able to help your SEO efforts. In most cases, the following formats for keywords seem to work well in optimizing the content of a real estate website:

- "name of the city" real estate

- "name of the city" homes for sale

- "name of the city + state abr" real estate

- "type of property" for sale in "name of the city"

- "type of property" for sale in "name of the city + state abr"

- "action + type of property" in "name of the city"

Those are just examples of how you can format your keywords. However, make sure to spend time studying the market completely before creating a list of keywords relevant to the real estate industry. That way, you can use those that can truly help you attain a higher ranking.

Build Content Specific to the City

You can also use Google SEO for real estate marketing by creating content specific to the city. This type of content should show not only in your blogs but also in your interviews and transcribed videos. Making your content city-specific can help make your website rank higher on Google. This technique may require plenty of research and a lot of time used for writing, publishing, and editing, but the effort is all worth it once you see the positive result.

You can also connect this strategy with the EAT concept, which signifies Expertise, Authority, and Trust. In this concept, Google tends to offer rewards to websites that have high EAT. If you want to increase your EAT, then show proof that you do indeed have authority in regards to the area.

You can achieve that by implementing local SEO. As a real estate agent, your goal is to fill your site with useful, actionable, and engaging content – content that is sure to provide relevant answers to everything that your prospects need to know about your city or area of focus. By doing that, you can encourage your target audience to trust your ability to provide them with only useful and relevant information through your website.

In this case, you have to be useful and local by ensuring that the content you create revolves around every city you intend to dominate. One thing to note is that there will always be cities that are easier to focus on compared to others. This usually depends on competition and search volume.

By producing this top-funnel content, you can open up your chances of capturing the interest of a user during the initial stages of their research. In case you are still unsure of what content to write about, the most recommended topics will be:

- City attractions and landmarks

- Top employers, jobs, and economy

- Neighborhoods

- Schools around the neighborhood

- Shopping and restaurants

- Things to do

- Transportation

All these topics are specific to the city, giving your target audience an idea about what to expect in case they purchase a property there.

Promote Mobile Optimization

Another effective SEO tip is to optimize your website so that your target audience can access it on their smartphones and mobile devices. Keep in mind that over half of the internet traffic globally is taken from mobile devices. It means that proving your worth to Google and satisfying customers with your content can be made possible by designing your website so that it can smoothly operate on tablets and smartphones.

If you are ready to optimize your site for mobile use, then prioritize key areas, including page and hosting speed, homepage, the responsiveness of the design, site search and navigation, conversions, forms, and usability. You will immediately know that you have successfully made your web design responsive if it makes automatic adjustments to fit the screen of any device. This level of responsiveness also contributes a lot to the overall usability of your site.

As for the speed, improve it as much as possible. Ensure that your web visitors will not wait too long to view your content. It should be speedy enough to prevent them from returning to the search results to look for other similar sites that are more user-friendly. An effective tip to increase the loading speed of each page is to keep everything simple yet attractive.

Also, ensure that the user does not have to exert too much effort or consume too much time navigating through your pages to get what they want. Otherwise, you can't expect a follow-through. If possible, use Google's mobile-friendly test tool. It is what you need to figure out whether your site passes the speed test. Aside from that, the tool can also provide you with information about any issues affecting the speed.

Speeding things up is also possible by minifying codes and optimizing images on your page. Also, take advantage of an emulator and use it to clearly see how your web content gets displayed across different mobile devices.

Take Advantage of Social Media Platforms

While social media does not directly impact your ranking on Google search engines, you can still expect it to play a vital role in your digital marketing technique. By tapping into social media, you will have an easier time connecting with your target audience. It also helps to boost your online exposure, establish trust, awareness, and authority, and drive conversions and website traffic.

Note that without social media accounts, you may find it challenging to obtain more online visibility. However, while you may be tempted to try all social media networks, it would be better if you just stick to a few platforms, particularly those with a higher reach. Do your best in the platforms you have chosen instead of spreading yourself too thin to the point that the quality of your content suffers.

Apart from Facebook and Instagram, which we have already discussed earlier, other social media platforms that seem to work well for real estate agents are Pinterest and Twitter. Make use of these social media platforms whenever you need to share videos, blog content, and other relevant details and information, like the latest news and statistics about your listings.

Pinterest and Instagram, for instance, are ideal for use whenever you need to promote your site using visuals. If you need to demonstrate your best sales and marketing opportunities, then consider doing them on Facebook.

Also, remember that every time you post and share content on your social media accounts, you need to integrate local-focused descriptions and hashtags. Incorporate geo-targeted keywords, too. That way, your social media posts will become more effective in expanding your reach.

Utilize Structured Data Markup

Otherwise called schema, structured data markup is essential as it allows Google, as well as other major search engines, to get to know more about the type of content your page focuses on. If you want your website to focus on displaying rich snippets, then ensure that you integrate them wherever possible.

Remember, though, that while snippets contribute a lot to improving the results of your SEO efforts, you may find it challenging to earn them. It will be a challenge to compete with huge real estate businesses, too.

In this case, do an extensive keyword search and look for long-tail keywords that perfectly suit your brand. Such keywords must have your geo-phrases, too. Produce the best content for such keywords and incorporate some of the top queries in Google into it, particularly in the form of headings. This works to significantly increase your Google ranking for such keywords.

When using structured data markup, you also have to remember that your real estate business will most likely benefit from RealEstateAgent, Product, RentAction, Place, Offer, PostalAddress, Residence, WebPage, and SearchResultsPage. Use one depending on the actual structure of your website.

If you still have no idea how and where to begin, as well as what you should use specifically, then consider seeking the help of an SEO professional. After adding a schema to your website, use Google's Structured Data Testing tool to determine how accurate it is.

Building a Quality Website for Long-term Success

Aside from the digital marketing strategies that we have already discussed, it is also a must to focus on creating a quality website – one that will be by your side right from the start of your career and help you attain your desired long-term success.

Building a quality website will always be a major factor in your digital marketing campaign. As a matter of fact, your goal of attaining success as a real estate agent through digital marketing will not be achievable without having your own website.

However, even if you are an incredible real estate agent, it does not necessarily mean that you also need to be extremely tech-savvy to create a website of your own. Remember that when you start your career, you will be busy finding properties to sell or showing homes and other properties to your target audience. You will also be spending a lot of your time marketing new listings and writing contracts. Plus, you will be attending training programs provided by your company to polish your real estate skills.

With that in mind, you may not have a lot of time to learn and improve your technical skills for website creation. Despite that, you can still build a website that reflects your business acumen while laying a strong foundation for your business. You only need a couple of things to make that happen – hosting and domain name.

Once these key components are in place, you can decide on whether you should make the website on your own or hire a website designer so you can have a real professional do it for you. In case you intend to be in complete control of the layout, design, and content of your site, then a DIY website builder specifically designed for the real estate niche is helpful for you. It is less expensive than hiring a custom web designer.

Buy a Domain Name

As mentioned earlier, a vital component of your real estate website is the domain name. It refers to the term/s typed by people into their browser's search bar to reach your website. An example would be godaddy.com. Buying a domain name is actually a pretty straightforward process. This is especially true if you make use of a legitimate and trusted registrar for domains.

Regardless of whether you buy the domain from GoDaddy or any other company, it is important to look for a registrar that meets the following requirements:

- ICANN accredited – The acronym stands for Internet Corp. for Assigned Names and Numbers. It is the governing body responsible for handling domain name registrars.

- Provides complete control over your chosen domain – Note that there are registrars that will that tend to retain partial control over the domain, which is why they can still add their contact details to certain parts of it. This may cause extreme difficulty in case you want to move to another registrar. It may also prevent you from directing your chosen domain to the hosting provider you prefer. With that said, avoid those with partial control. Ensure that your control over the domain is full.

- Offers quality support whenever necessary – Your chosen registrar needs to be around to guide you during the troubleshooting process in case something goes wrong. You should be able to receive quality support whenever problems with the domain arise.

You can detect the ability of the registrar to offer quality support by verifying the availability of their customer service before your final purchase. With timely and quality support, you can avoid the risk of missing valuable traffic opportunities, leads, and prospective clients just because there is a registrar problem.

- Provides additional pricing and options for the domain – When building a website, the domain is probably not your biggest expense throughout the process. As a matter of fact, you can already access the majority of domain extensions for just less than $20 annually.

  However, you have to check out the additional pricing and options provided by a particular registrar before picking it. The reason is that you need to consider other features, such as automatic renewal, domain privacy, and theft protection.

Once you decide on where you should buy the domain name, it is time to select the perfect one for your website. Note that the domain name selection process may be the hardest part associated with building a quality website for your real estate career and business. You can simplify the process, though, with these guidelines:

- Pick a short yet memorable domain name – Remember that the domain name you have selected is not somewhere to use puns. If you want to use puns, it would be better to save those during an open house event. The domain needs to be short so that people can easily remember, spell, and say it.

You will be using this domain name throughout your digital marketing campaigns. You may even have to incorporate it into radio ads, bus shelter ads, and other promotional materials. With that said, go for one that people can easily recall.

- Integrate your location into it – This is valuable not only for your clients but also for search engines. For instance, if you want to focus on selling real estate properties in Florida, then indicate that in your domain name. That way, you can avoid having to deal with queries for areas that are not part of your focus. Some examples of location-based extensions for domain names are "boston," "la," and "nyc."

- Take advantage of new extensions – This tip is helpful, especially if the area of your focus does not have an extension based specifically on location yet. If that is the case, it would be best to use your creativity to find other new extensions that you can integrate into the domain. Among the extensions you can use nowadays would be "forsale," "house," "rent," and "casa."

- Pick a distinctive and unique one – You may be tempted to follow the footsteps of a competitor who seems to be doing well right now, but you should avoid doing that, especially when picking the perfect domain for your site. You have to showcase your site's uniqueness.

Note that with the numerous real estate agents vying for attention online, you need to look for a way to be unique and distinctive. You need to stand out so you will continue receiving queries from your target audience and encourage them to do business with you. You can make that happen by integrating unique elements into your website, including your brand and domain names.

When it comes to deciding and selecting a domain name, make a list of options. Create a shortlist of prospective domain names so you can identify the ones currently available. The problem is that you can't always determine the availability of a particular domain if you only plug it into your browser.

The reason is that there are instances when even owned domains open up a page that says "site not found." This usually happens when the owner of the domain was not able to complete the building of his website.

To determine the availability of your selected domain names, you may want to use the search tool for domains offered by GoDaddy. Just input the domain you prefer to use in the site's search bar. Doing that will cause either two possible scenarios – one is that it may show that the domain is available. If that is the case, then expect to be prompted to finish the registration of the domain so you can finally add it to the cart.

The second scenario would be that the domain is already owned. In that case, expect to receive a list containing suggested domains that are quite similar to the one you chose earlier. It is at your discretion to pick one domain from the list.

Just make sure that your choice meets the requirements and criteria mentioned earlier. Alternatively, you can begin a new search using another unique domain name from the list you created. You can continue doing that until you find a domain that is available and is a good fit for your company.

Choose a Web Hosting Provider

The next key component that you have to focus on when trying to build a quality website is the web host. The entire selection process may be overwhelming and tricky initially, but with the help of these factors, you can arrive at the best decision:

- Security – Ensure that you look for a web hosting provider that gives your website the highest level of security. Review the things offered by the web hosts in your list thoroughly, especially when it comes to protection from hacks and viruses. Also, spend time checking out details regarding their security certifications and daily backups.

  Another important piece of information to check out is the process used when restoring your site in case it gets damaged. A good web host is capable of providing website owners, like you, with superior security.

- Software – Another thing you should remember about web hosts is that you can't expect all of them to be created equally. With that in mind, you really have to check out what software they offer. Determine if partnering with a particular web host will require you to use additional software so you can make your properties available online.

  Any software you need must be available with the web host you are thinking of using. For instance, find out whether the web hosting provider offers software and optimization features capable of boosting the speed of your site.
- Support – Choose a web hosting provider who can provide you with excellent support too. Make sure that you can easily contact their technical support team any time of the day. Get a complete understanding of the kind of support that your chosen hosting plan provides, especially if you want to avoid downtime as much as possible.

- Extra or additional features – In case you are still confused as to who you should choose from the web hosting providers in your list, try to compare them based on their extra or additional features. Find out which one offers extra features that you can truly use.

Some web hosts provide built-in themes, site builders, staging sites, and design tools – all of which can help in building a quality website. Pick one based on who can provide you with most, if not all, of the features you truly need.

Install a Theme

This is another vital step in building a quality website for your real estate business. The entire process actually involves not only the installation but also the purchasing, activation, and validation of the new design theme you have chosen.

One thing to note when it comes to building your real estate website is that researching the best design theme/s may take you several days. The good news is that once you have made your choice, it only takes around 15 to 20 minutes for you to buy, install, activate, and then validate it.

Choosing a design theme is something that you have to think of carefully. Remember that it will serve as the blueprint of your website. It will provide details on the exact places where the elements of your site will go.

The theme will also serve as a guide on how to structure everything within your website. For instance, it will serve as the basis of the standard font you will be using, whether you will have a picture in the page header/s or not, or if you are going to add a menu at the bottom portion of the homepage. These may just be small details, but your chosen design theme will be able to handle them.

One of the most highly recommended design themes for real estate professionals nowadays is the WP Residence. Many recommend it because of its flexibility, allowing you to customize and adjust the settings of each offered theme to make your website look fully customized. It also has a good track record, which shows that users have found it to be good to work with.

Apart from that, it has most, if not all, of the features and functionality you are hoping to get from a design theme. It allows you to do everything that you want to with your site, such as advanced property searches, user log-ins, floor plans, and payment collection systems. Moreover, WP Residence is affordable and has themes that are truly responsive and ready for mobile use.

You also have other options when it comes to the design theme. While picking other providers may cause slight differences in the purchase, activation, and installation processes, you can still expect the basic structure to stay the same.

After installing your theme, the majority of your work will start taking place on your website, particularly if what you are using is WordPress. You may find it intimidating initially due to the many menus integrated there, but you'll get used to using them eventually.

The first thing you will most likely see is the long toolbar that runs down the screen's left-hand side. There is also a short toolbar, which runs across the top. Those are the menus that will let you access all the features on the site.

Install Helpful Plug-Ins

Once you already have a theme set up, it is time to choose some plug-ins guaranteed to help to improve the value of your website. Plug-ins are crucial to boosting your website's functionality. If you want to have an easier time managing property listings while making them more appealing to your prospects, then check out some plug-ins and figure out which ones can help to design your website.

An example of a plug-in that is extremely useful for real estate agents is Estatik. It has several vital features, like property wish lists and savable searches. You can also find multiple widget options here. Furthermore, it provides a customizable search function, slideshow function, and information request forms.

If you are on a budget, then Easy Property Listings is a low-risk plug-in you can use. It is affordable yet highly effective to boost the functionality of the website you have created. You will love the dynamic nature of this plug-in. It is also feature-heavy, with most of its features designed to make your website look better.

What is even great about Easy Property Listings is that it provides a user-friendly solution when it comes to getting your listings online quickly and in a straightforward manner. It has more than seven customized post types and 150 custom fields. You can, therefore, rest assured that you don't need developer skills just to build your site in the specific manner you intend to.

With the help of this plug-in, your visitors can sort your listings based on certain categories, like price, location, and date. You can also flag individual listings as under contract, sold, or any other category. Moreover, it does not set any limitations as to the number of listings on your site.

You can still find a lot of useful plug-ins for real estate websites like yours. Just figure out which ones you really need as well as the ones guaranteed to make the experience of your target audience better whenever they visit your site.

Prioritize the Core Features

Now that you have integrated the basic foundation for your website, it is time to learn about the core features you have to prioritize. Note that for you to compete in the somewhat competitive real estate business, you have to make your website as appealing as possible and include the core features that you and your target audience will find useful.

One important reminder, though, is that for a web design to be effective, it must adhere to a few principles – among which are a customer-centered approach, mobile-friendliness, and responsiveness. Now that we have those principles out in the open, here are the core features we are talking about:

- Property listings – One feature you should focus on when designing your website is the section where you can show your property listings. Note that if you do not have this feature, your website will not stand out from the others. To let your prospects check what your available offers are upon their visit, you need to embed listings on the homepage layout.

You may also want to showcase your expertise by incorporating relevant information regarding any successfully closed deals. That way, your potential clients can see you as someone whom they can completely trust. There should also be a section on your website that shows your featured offers – the ones that you consider as the best out of all your proposals.

Include some features that will allow your visitors to save their preferred properties as favorites. Meanwhile, in case there are homes they do not like, they also need to have an option to hide them.

- Visuals – You also have to focus on the website's visuals. After all, your goal will always be to capture the attention of your target audience and convert them into leads. You can only achieve that if you make the site's visuals as appealing as possible. Focus on posting eye-catching photography on your site. It can help establish the overall atmosphere while encouraging your prospects to purchase properties from you.

Also, remember that the first impression will always last, so you have to capture the attention of your visitors the moment they open your website. You can also achieve that by filling your real estate platform with professional-looking and attractive high-resolution pictures of properties that you have for lease or sale.

Aside from pictures, you can also incorporate video content into your website. Add such content in the Homepage's main block. This type of content can boost the appeal of your website even further.

- Registration – In building a real estate website, remind yourself how important it is to integrate a registration feature. This specific feature is necessary as it can significantly influence the buying decisions of your prospect.

  With a registration feature around, your visitors will have a personal area, which is helpful to earn their interest as it shows that you care for them and you are willing to add value to what you are offering.

  A nice idea would be to integrate advanced functionality into the user accounts of your visitors. These should include instant support, mortgage calculators, and saved search results. Keep in mind that most online users do not like the idea of filling out signup forms that are too long. They do not like to undertake complex steps, either.

  To avoid veering them away from your website, integrate a feature that allows them to use their social media accounts for registration. You can just request additional information and details later on.

- Lead capture forms and call-to-action – The lead capture form and your call-to-action are also two of the most important features that you have to integrate into your website. You need to create an eye-catching call-to-action, one that will encourage your visitors to take action.

  You also need to provide them with an enticing subscription or lead capture forms. However, you have to incorporate both these features in your site correctly. For instance, when you design your site's internal pages and Homepage, set a limit to the number of CTAs each page must have. The rule of thumb is to avoid letting each page contain over two CTAs.

- Every button and link on the page should also be clickable. They need to direct your visitors to the right pages. Also, remember that to build a site capable of satisfying even those demanding online users, you should try emulating a hot trend in web design. Some examples would be transparent buttons and natural shapes.

  As far as the lead capture forms are concerned, your goal is to keep them short. Also, integrate a sort of promise – one that you can surely fulfill. That way, you can encourage them to fill out the form. The promise could be in the form of a free e-book or a newsletter or more details of a property once they provide you with their email address.

- Contact us page – Show your visitors that they can easily reach and access you. You can do that by integrating a contact us page. Regardless of whether you decide to add a separate page for the Contact Us section or a live chat section providing instant support, the goal is for your prospects to reach and access you anytime without any hassle.

  A wise tip is to add a contact us page to your menu. It should be in the navigation bar. You may also add a sticky pop-up together with the live chat function. If you want, you can even choose to add a map showing the exact location of your office along with the actual address. Apart from giving your visitors an idea regarding your physical location, it also reassures them that your company truly exists, thereby earning their trust.

  You may also want to integrate a get-in-touch button or form on your site's footer, though some users may not be fond of scrolling down to the bottom. If you want this button or form to become more visible, add it to the user dashboards.

- Blog – Another crucial element in your website that will surely improve its overall quality is the blog. As a matter of fact, a lot of real estate agents believe that it should be part of a newbie's to-do list when it is time for them to create their own site.

However, you also have to remember that not all sites that focus on property buying and selling require a blog. This means you have to figure out first whether you truly need this specific page. Find out if it will truly be helpful for you.

If you are one hundred percent sure that your main audience is waiting for you to begin sharing your valuable content, then it would be wise for you to start a blog section. You may also want to include a blog section on your website if you have plans of attracting new leads and prospects through content marketing.

If you decide to add a blog to your website, then remember that a lot of online readers love it when they interact with you or with each other. That said, it would be a plus to include a comments section beneath every blog post. It will be a way for you to hear their thoughts about your posts and interact with them.

- Searchability function – This should help your web visitors easily search for whatever they need to find on the site. However, this does not just involve a simple search box, which allows users to type in something to scan your site. It should be a feature that will help the majority of users when searching for something like they do in real life.

For instance, there is a great likelihood for online users to prefer properties within certain areas and within specific price ranges. There are even those who want to pick a property based on the number of rooms it has or whether it has a garage.

In that case, your site should have a searchability function in the sense that they can find specific answers. One example would be a suggestion box that can be prompted whenever a user clicks or types something on the search bar.

However, remember that while extensiveness is crucial in this step, you should still avoid inundating visitors with too many drop-down boxes. Only choose the key elements to avoid confusing your visitors and preventing them from looking for other sites to find what they need.

Apart from the above-mentioned core elements, you can also make sure that the website you create is of top-notch quality with these additional tips:

Make it Mobile-Friendly

Build your site in such a way that it is mobile-friendly. It should be designed in such a way so that it will not look terrible even when displayed on a mobile device. Note that the small sizes of mobile devices may cause standard websites to not present well on the screen.

Still, you can do something to make it look the same way as when you open it on a bigger screen. Fortunately, if you are using WordPress, you can access various themes that can automatically help you to boost the mobile-friendliness of your site. Most of these are referred to as responsive themes.

Focus on Comprehensiveness

Even if you still consider yourself a newbie real estate agent, you are probably aware of the needs of the majority of your target audience. Those requirements and needs are even your basis when making and delivering your sales pitches. You have to transmit such knowledge to your site, which is why you need it to be as comprehensive as possible.

Aside from providing information about the actual property, make a point of offering your visitors other supporting details comprehensively. Some additional details they would like to know are education zones, nearby amenities, and highways.

If you are planning to tap into the interest of investors, then be comprehensive as well. Provide them with relevant market reports as the data there will probably capture their interest.

Ensure That Your Site Supports Quick Follow-Ups

In addition to having an appealing site design and providing plenty of useful information, you also need to allow quick follow-ups in order to hook your target audience. You can do that by providing several convenient options when contacting you.

This may come in the form of a call-to-action displayed in a bright red button that they can easily click. It could also be a link directing them to your email so they can easily send their inquiries. Make sure to put these features in a spot on your website where you think your prospects are already deciding to contact you.

There are definitely many things that you can do to improve the quality of your website. Just make sure that you prioritize the core elements. Also, once your website is already set up, apply the Google SEO tips that we have discussed earlier. All those tips can make your website recognizable in the online world. Aside from that, do not forget to integrate social media marketing as it is one of the most powerful and effective marketing techniques right now.

How to Generate Leads with Third-Party Websites

In addition to all the digital marketing techniques that we have already covered, you may also want to take advantage of legitimate and reliable third-party websites to generate leads. Note that even if you already have your own website, you can't expect it to give you the number of leads you want all the time.

In that case, you need to seek the help of lead generation companies focusing on real estate. These companies can assist real estate agents like you in capturing, organizing, and nurturing new leads until they are fully prepared to sell or purchase a property.

Just make sure to pick a company that can truly be a major contributor to your success. Compare them based not only on price but also on customer support, ease of use, as well as built-in features, like blogging, email marketing automation, and IDX integration.

Some companies and third-party websites that you can tap are the following:

Realtor.com

By partnering with realtor.com, you get the chance to acquire leads from prospective buyers who are actively in search of a property in your market. The good thing about this third-party website is that it has several features and has software designed to help real estate agents like you to capture, connect, and communicate with such leads.

It offers lead generation opportunities at paid and free levels. You can even take advantage of its impressive tools that have been proven to be useful to generate and nurture leads capable of filling your pipeline. Another advantage of realtor.com is that it has already made a name and an excellent reputation for itself.

As a matter of fact, it ranks second of the biggest real estate marketplaces online, thanks to its more than 60,000,000 visitors monthly. With that said, it is safe to say that it is indeed a powerful platform for boosting your presence online and making your business more established.

Realtor.com offers leads under a 1-year contract. However, you can also generate leads here that you can work on for six months. Such leads are derived from the use of free services. There are also those that you can optimize by choosing to subscribe to the company's paid options. If you choose this option, then expect to pay at least $25 per month for the service.

One thing to note regarding the pricing of realtor.com is that it is often based on the values of the homes belonging to a particular zip code. If you target more expensive areas, then expect the leads here to be more expensive.

You may want to invest in a specific zip code where you are working so you can obtain exclusivity. However, remember that it is more expensive, prompting you to shell out around a thousand dollars every month. Also, remember that the majority of the zip codes right now have already been purchased, which means you still have to wait for a while before you can use the good ones.

Avoid going for the most inexpensive choice, though. Do not settle on a zip code you don't like just because it is cheap. Stick to what you like and just try improving your lead generation efforts with the help of realtor.com.

To gain the best returns on your investment on realtor.com in the form of leads, you may want to follow these tips:

- Maximize the use of your profile page – Use it to the fullest so you can market your business more effectively. Your profile page should contain your headshot, bio, and contact information. It also has to contain recently closed and present listings. Your profile needs to have reviews and recommendations, too. All these details can make you look as trustworthy as possible to your audience.

- Choose the perfect headshot – Remember that it is the first thing that your prospects will see. With that said, you need to use a headshot that is capable of conveying trust, confidence, and competence. Integrate elements designed to leave a good impression regarding your business and brand, like the right background, professional attire, and smiling aura.

- Include positive reviews and testimonials – You can also stand out regardless of the many real estate agents on realtor.com by including positive reviews and testimonials in your profile. Remember that client reviews serve as social proof that you are indeed good at what you are doing. This can contribute a lot to your successful lead generation efforts.

Zillow

Another third-party website that you can use to generate leads is Zillow. Just build your real estate agent profile on Zillow, and you will be able to take full advantage of the website's help to boost your ability to generate leads. The good thing about Zillow is that it is free. You can also easily set up your profile on the Zillow group.

Apart from that, it is capable of exposing your skills, expertise, and information to millions of its visitors every month. Right after setting up your Zillow profile, you can start taking advantage of it by generating leads through various means – among which are the following:

- Make your Zillow profile the best source of local information about real estate –Ensure that your profile is full of information that both sellers and buyers of real estate will find useful and valuable. Offer links and information on local stuff, like the weather, transportation, local resources, local events, and schools, among many others.

  Your goal is to show your prospects that you are indeed an expert in that specific area. By showing that you are a helpful resource, you can easily turn them into actual clients. One way to improve your Zillow profile is to include short yet creative videos.

  Aside from profiling your real estate listings, you can also post videos that showcase the local expertise. Videos focusing on customer testimonials and neighborhood explorations can also make your profile thrive.

- Take advantage of the ideal team association or agent – If you are a part of a team, then you can rest assured that Zillow is capable of providing a certain association you can use to communicate it to anyone who views your listings and profile. While you can find several team members who improperly display themselves as a single conjoined profile to simplify account management, it may still be a bad idea in case you have a listing that is not existing on the other team member's page.

It may lead to a few data issues. Therefore, if you are part of a team, ensure that you still have your own profile on Zillow. After establishing your account, you can finally take advantage of the team association function as a means of letting Zillow, as well as your visitors, learn about the team you are associated or affiliated with.

- Correct the data in your listings – Make sure that all your listings in Zillow are highly accurate. Remember that this third-party site completely and heavily relies on the data it derives from users and sources. With that, there is a high chance of incomplete and inaccurate data. It is the reason why you should avoid relying too much on the information being fed on Zillow when creating your listings.

Spend time writing informative and creative descriptions for every property. Fill up all fields and upload images and videos that are both professionally shot and creative. If there are inaccuracies, correct them right away. That way, it will be accurate enough to the point that you will not have a hard time generating the trust of your targeted leads.

- Include the properties you sold in the past – Remember that your prospects, especially property sellers, would like to know the kinds of properties you have successfully sold in the past. Most of them would even like to find out how much the property was sold for compared to the initial cost in its listing. To attract these prospective clients, try adding as many of the listings you sold in the past as possible.

  Just navigate to your account's sales history page so you can upload or check your listings. Ensure that you verify all the info regarding your sold properties to assure your leads of their accuracy.

- Answer questions – It is also easy for you to establish your web or online presence and acquire leads in the process by showing proof that you are indeed a reliable resource of information. In that case, take advantage of the website's Zillow Advice feature. This specific page shows how useful a resource you are as it lets you create an open forum involving everyone involved in a given transaction.

  Here, you can answer questions thrown at you. It can improve your authority and reliability in the industry, thereby encouraging your prospects and leads to get in touch with you.

Other Third-Party Websites for Real Estate Lead Generation

Apart from realtor.com and Zillow, you can also take advantage of the following third-party websites when it comes to generating leads for your real estate business.

- Propertybase – With a powerful website platform, a highly effective engine for driving prospects, and a customizable and versatile customer relationship management (CRM) tool, Propertybase will help you succeed in the real estate industry. The good thing about this website is that it is consumer-centric. This means that it is built to satisfy consumers down to the tiniest details.

  It even gives real estate agents the chance to customize the prefilled fields or portions of their IDX search. With that, you can certainly improve your ability to meet and connect with the specific requirements of the target customers you intend to serve.

- Real Geeks – You can also take advantage of Real Geeks. One reason why this site is so successful is that it holds a truly versatile platform, which works well for small teams, brokerages, and solo real estate agents alike. It features its IDX website with a versatile front-end editor, allowing real estate agents to customize it based on the feel and look they prefer.

Another reason to like Real Geeks is that it provides incredible pricing choices. For $249 monthly, you can already get its basic website and customer relationship management tool – both of which can provide you with a lot of things that will maximize your experience on Real Geeks. You may also spend a few dollars more monthly so you can take advantage of the expertise and skills of Real Geeks when it comes to Google and Facebook advertising.

- Placester – If you are part of NAR (National Association of Realtors), then you are fully qualified to use the Placester website, which is famous for its impressive IDX feed and its amazing options for basic lead capture. What is great about Placester is that you can get such features for only $64 monthly. This site even provides several amazing options and features for new real estate professionals, particularly those who are still on a budget.

The package you will be getting from Placester is also more than enough as it already includes a website that is not only mobile-friendly, but that also has IDX integration capability. You can also get home valuation landing pages and a blog platform, among many others.

If you are working with a team, then you may want to take advantage of its advanced plan. This plan can provide you with luxe design features, advanced lead capture, and lead routing, among many other advanced and modern features.

- Chime – Another highly effective lead generation website that works well for real estate agents is Chime. An advantage of this website is that it offers a unique yet easy-to-follow solution for your real estate website requirements. It also gives you access to a full-bodied CRM tool, so you can conveniently follow up with your captured leads.

Another thing that makes a website powered by Chime so impressive is that it instantly shows that it is a place for home valuation and property searches. It is beneficial, especially if you look at it from a lead generation perspective. Every time your prospects get into your page, they will no longer wonder what is going to be their next step. This results in a significant increase in the leads in your funnel, which will most likely happen quickly. We have only mentioned a few of the many third-party websites you can use for your real estate lead generation campaigns. You can always tap in to get their help whenever you feel like you still need more professional assistance for digital marketing. Just make sure to spend time studying all your options so you can pick a reliable and trustworthy website guaranteed to offer you the help that you specifically need.

Chapter 3
Sales Prospecting

Sales prospecting is also one of the skills that a new real estate agent should master. The reason is that prospecting will always be the first vital step you need to take during the sales process. It is what you need to go through when identifying prospective clients then interacting with them, so you can convert them into your actual leads and clients.

As a real estate agent, your success will most likely be dependent on acquiring new clients. The problem is that you can't expect such clients to fall into your lap without working hard to generate them. It would be great for real estate agents to have clients who are constantly seeking their help, and prospecting -otherwise referred to as farming - is often a major contributor to that.

As a matter of fact, this process takes a huge chunk of how real estate agents spend their time. In other words, you will not just be doing general marketing designed to put your brand out there. You also have to work on targeting certain areas, neighborhoods, homes and properties so you can find your next clients – and that is where knowledge about prospecting can be of help.

Through prospecting, you can convince a homeowner to sell his house even if it is not on the market yet. You just have to provide them with the right information and demonstrate appropriate circumstances. So basically, prospecting is a vital means to find both seller and buyer leads without waiting for a long time for them to find you.

Importance of Prospecting

Even with the modern marketing techniques available at present, sales prospecting still works for a lot of real estate agents. When done correctly, it can create a pipeline filled with prospective customers. This means that by prospecting effectively, you will always have a steady and stable flow of client listings.

Apart from that, it makes it possible for you to position yourself in the industry as a trusted and reliable advisor. It gives you the chance to focus on proper accounts. With that in mind, it is truly necessary to gain a full understanding of how prospecting fits into the entire sales cycle. You also need to be disciplined enough to do prospecting regularly.

If you only spend your entire time focusing on listings, then it is highly likely that you will end up running out of properties to buy and sell. As a new agent aiming to attain success, remind yourself of the importance of setting aside a certain portion of your time doing prospecting activities every week. You may also want to build a database of your existing and prospective clients.

Once you successfully sell a client's property, you can also expect them to assist you in future prospecting by recommending your services. This makes this step even more beneficial as it can help to attract more and more leads and clients through referrals and testimonials.

Understanding Numbers and Ratios When Prospecting

When it comes to prospecting, numbers, and ratios are extremely important. After all, this entire process will always be a numbers game. You need to know and completely understand your numbers and ratios, as these will help you set a more realistic goal. One thing to focus on, in this case, is to establish a daily goal on the specific number of new contacts you intend to reach.

According to NAR (National Association of Realtors), the usual rate of lead-to-transaction conversion for agents is around 1% (around 0.4% to 1.2% in the majority of cases). This means that for every 100 prospects you contact or communicate with, only around 1 to 2 of them will actually be converted into clients. With that figure, consider setting a realistic goal – one that will not pressure you too much, especially if you are still a beginner.

As a new real estate agent, you may thrive with around five contacts daily. As soon as you gain more experience, you can increase this to around 10 to 15 contacts. You have a higher chance of reaching that figure once you become more experienced and gain more confidence in what you do.

Apart from the usual rate of lead-to-transaction conversion, you also have to take into accounts the following percentages:

- Around 48% of people do not send follow-ups to a prospect

- Around 25% stop and contact the prospect for the second time

- Around 12% of sales agents only make three contacts and then stop

- Around 125 sales agents acquire over three contacts

- Only around 20% of your sales come from four contacts or less

With these percentages, it is safe to say that following up is necessary for every prospecting task. Also, remember that only around 80 percent of the sales of real estate agents are derived from around 5-12 contacts, which is quite low, triggering most of them to quit early. You should avoid committing the same mistake of quitting, though.

Improve your mindset about the way you look at prospecting. The reason is that your persistence will eventually give you the results you want. Persist on learning everything that you can about ratios and numbers, and eventually, you can improve yours and enjoy better figures that may also indicate your success.

It also helps to compute the specific number of prospects you should contact so you can lock down a seller or buyer's listing appointment. Most seasoned agents actually recommend the typical five contacts daily for newbies. This should be a great start. Apart from that, you also have to aim to secure one lead daily and one listing appointment weekly.

Make it a point to talk to your broker about this, though. Discuss the standard or average number that the firm is aiming for. While acquiring new clients requires hard work, you can also rely on your brokerage firm for help, especially when setting goals and following certain procedures.

Also, do not beat yourself up too much even if you do not hit the initial numbers and ratios that you have set yourself to achieve. Remind yourself that you are still new, and just like a lot of people, it may still be necessary for you to have a warm-up period so you can gather more confidence and boost your prospecting skills. During this time, it would be helpful to set manageable goals at first.

How to Use Phone Scripts in Prospecting

Undoubtedly, phone calls can contribute a lot to the success of your sales prospecting efforts. As a matter of fact, cold calling is perhaps one of the most effective and famous sales prospecting techniques capable of reaching the ones you are targeting. It is also easy to transform your supposed-to-be cold call intentions at first into warm ones after using the "Go Online" prospecting technique correctly.

Basically, cold calling refers to a method that involves interacting with new prospects by calling them and then pitching what you are offering to them. If you plan to implement this approach, then remember that the manner through which you acquire the phone numbers can have a significant impact on the rate of your success.

Also, remember that proper research and preparation are necessary. Many seasoned real estate agents also discovered that emailing before cold calling is an effective strategy that produces much better results. The reason is that the email also acts as an excuse for making the call while offering relevant details regarding your product or company before your actual call.

Regardless of who you want to reach, it is safe to say that calling prospects is definitely a cost-effective solution when it comes to reaching out and discussing the needs and requirements of a prospective buyer or client. Phone calls also seem to be beneficial for real estate agents, particularly those who want to be more personal with their prospects.

Aside from that, calling your prospects via phone will allow both of you to have a natural conversation regarding the real estate market in your locality. You can also do it at a time that is most convenient for the two of you.

Do you want to start using phone calls to get in touch with your prospects? Then make sure you prepare the perfect phone scripts for the right situations. Note that if you intend to use a script for your cold calls, practicing beforehand can greatly help.

With proper practice, you have a higher chance of impressing your new prospects, thereby helping you attain your key objectives of interacting with them, including establishing rapport or trust, gathering information, and securing a follow-up. It is even possible to secure such a follow-up without facing the drawbacks of contacting your prospects via the phone, like the possibility of them hanging up, perceiving the whole process as impersonal, and increasing the risk of calling your prospects at inconvenient times.

While cold calling seems to be frightening at first, you can always seek the help of well-prepared phone scripts to lessen your discomfort. Some examples of phone scripts that will work on specific situations are the following:

To Follow Up on Your Email

It is always a great idea to send an email to a prospect before calling, as it offers an incredible opening for the conversation. It can also create a sort of familiarity, especially if your target client has already read your email and gained some background information regarding your product, service, or the company you are working with.

Example:

Good day _____ (name of your prospect)!

This is _____ (your name) representing _____ (name of the company you are affiliated with).

I am calling you to follow up on your response regarding the email we sent about _____ (the focus of the sent email or product's actual value to your prospect). Do you find it interesting?

I understand that you are busy, but would you be willing to spare a few minutes to answer a few questions from us? That way, we will understand your specific needs and requirements better. – (This should prompt your conversation. Gather as much information as you can during this time)

Are you free on _____ (day) at around _____ (time) so we can discuss the business even further?

To Call/Contact a Referral

If your actual clients refer you to new prospects, particularly those that they know, creating trust between you and your new prospects will be a lot easier. The reason is that they already heard about you from someone they know. This means that you also have a higher chance of receiving a positive reception.

You may want to ask those who are part of your social network and present their customer base to refer you to the people they know. You can then use the following sample script:

Example:

Good day _____ (name of prospect)!

This is _____ (your name) representing _____ (name of the company you are affiliated with).

I was able to get a hold of your contact number through _____ (name of the person who referred you) – Make sure to also indicate how you are related to the person who referred you to your new prospect here as well as what makes them think your product is valuable.

Is it something you are interested in? Would you be willing to spare a few minutes to talk about what I am offering even further? – Try having a good conversation here so you can gather additional relevant information.

May I ask for your email address so I can formally send my proposal and set a schedule for our follow-up meeting, depending on your most convenient time?

For Expired Listings

One thing to remember about expired listings is that cold calling under this scenario can be challenging and tricky. The reason is that the homeowner may have already talked to many real estate agents. There are even instances when they talk to different agents on a similar day. With that in mind, you have to prepare a great script – one that will let you stand out regardless of the fierce competition.

Good day! I'm _____ (your name) with _____ (company).

I am the real estate agent working around the neighborhood, and I just discovered that your home/property is no longer available for sale. Are you interested in putting your home back on the market? – Wait for your prospect's response. Sometimes, they may respond with "not for a while" or "maybe in the future."

I know that you may feel a bit disappointed since it is a nice house. Do you have any idea why the house did not sell? Did you have any other offers? – Listen intently to the response.

I was actually surprised to discover that it is still on the market after _____ days. I thought that a buyer would snatch it from the market in just a few weeks. Do you have specific reasons for selling the house? Where do you plan to move to?

I am sure many people have already contacted you. But as I mentioned a while ago, I have worked around this neighborhood for _____ years. I already know most of the details about this neighborhood and have successfully sold properties here. If you would like to give me a chance, I am proposing to help you sell your home. I am also interested in taking a tour of your home, at the very least, so we can figure out the reasons why it may not have caught the interest of buyers.

Would you be interested if I visit the place on _____ (day) at _____ (time)? You may also suggest the most convenient day and time for you. I am more than happy and willing to provide you with some feedback.

For FSBO Prospects

A lot of real estate agents believe that the best leads that they can contact for cold calling are the FSBO (For Sale by Owners) prospects. These are sellers who have probably informed the world about their interest to sell now or anytime soon. You should try to convince these prospects that they will need help when selling properties, and the perfect person to contact is you.

However, be prepared for their possible objections when you call them and convince them that they need your help. Common questions and objections you may hear would be "Why would you like to sell FSBO?" and "We want to save money."

In that case, here is a sample script you can use.

Good day! I'm _____ (your name) with _____ (company). I just found out that you still have a house that's available for sale in the neighborhood/area I am working on? Is the property still available?

Yes.

That's good to hear. Do you work with real estate agents?

No.

Okay, I am actually very knowledgeable about the area, so I'm wondering about your asking price for the house? If I can provide you with a buyer that perfectly agrees with the price, would you find that helpful?

Yes.

Great. I am really interested in scheduling a visit so I can check your house and figure out if it is a good fit for my client/s. I also wish to share some tips that can help FSBOs. Are you interested in scheduling a meeting at your most convenient time? Maybe this afternoon or tomorrow?

**** Possible objection: I am not really planning to work with a real estate agent. I do not want to spend money on a 5 to 6 percent commission. ****

Sure, I understand that. As a matter of fact, around ninety percent of FSBOs I have interacted with say the same. But if I can provide you with a means of netting a similar amount or possibly more by taking advantage of our services, would you be interested in working with us? – Wait for the response and ask for their reason for selling the house and the timeline for selling.

Okay, great. Would you be interested in scheduling a meeting? I would really love to find out whether I can sell the house for you within your given timeframe. Rest assured that I will be completely honest with you during the meeting. I will let you know right away whether I can or can't do it. Is that fine with you?

Yes.

Great. I truly appreciate that. Would you like to set our meeting at 4 pm this afternoon?

Additional Tips When Cold Calling

Apart from preparing phone scripts before you ever contact a prospect, make sure to also follow these additional tips and tricks when cold calling:

- Use the actual name of the prospect – You also have to introduce yourself right away. Greeting them by name and telling them about who you are and the company you are affiliated with can put them at ease and can greatly improve their receptiveness.

- Ask if you have called at your prospect's convenient time – Do not forget to ask whether the time you make the call is also convenient for them to speak. Just ask them politely if they are willing to spare a few minutes to speak with you. It shows how respectful you are of your prospects. It can also leave an impression that you are an agent who values the time of your prospects.

- Get straight to the point – Remember that cold calling is all about capturing the interest of your prospects and collecting information. It should not be all about providing information about the entire track record and history of your company. Try to keep the conversation short and provide only enough details about your offer. It should just be enough to stir the interest of your prospects, thereby making future meetings a necessity.

- Conduct proper research – The amount of research you will be doing, in this case, will greatly depend on the reason for calling your prospects. You need to keep all important notes in front of you so you will always have something to refer to in case there are certain details you forget on the spot. If you are calling a referral provided by one of your happy and satisfied clients, then be sure you include that fact during the call as it can help you build an instant connection.

- Practice your responses based on different scenarios – This means practicing various responses based on how they also respond to you. By rehearsing various outcomes when doing your call, you will not be surprised in cases where things do not go as you initially planned.

- Focus on being genuine – Remember that your prospects will want to feel like they are dealing with an agent who can genuinely take care of their needs. To achieve that, you should focus on establishing a personal connection. In fact, you need to show how genuine you are when building a connection instead of focusing too much on leaving an impression by bragging about your recent successful sales.

- End your call with a certain invitation – It could be inviting your prospects to an open house that will be happening soon. The usual invitation you can make, though, is a personal meeting so you can talk about the services you are offering.

- Secure the next step or follow-up – Never wait for your prospects to request a meeting, email, or any other information they may need to reach your goal. You should be the one to open it up but in a respectful manner.

With proper preparation, cold calling will become easier. The most important tip of all will always be having your phone scripts ready, so you can spontaneously talk to your prospects and build their trust and confidence in your ability.

How to Stay in Touch with Your Prospects

When it comes to prospecting, you need to find out exactly how you can continue keeping in touch with your prospects, particularly those who have a higher chance of getting converted into actual paying clients. Fortunately, it is not that hard to stay in touch with them nowadays as there are already various tools you can use in connecting with them.

In this case, you can apply these tips:

- Communicate with your previously happy and satisfied clients – You should still be in touch with them as it might help you get repeat business and gain referrals. The good thing about being referred to is that it can produce powerful and favorable results. Many even consider it the most powerful method of word-of-mouth marketing. The reason is a lot of people tend to trust what their trusted friends and family recommend to them instead of the other sources.

- Send a direct mail or email – You can also stay in touch with your prospects by sending them either direct mail or email. The goal here is to try communicating with them through various means, making them aware that you are around whenever they need the help of a real estate agent.

The good thing about this approach is that it lets you remain on top in the minds of your previous clients and prospects. Just ensure that your messages are personalized, so the recipients will enjoy receiving them. Also, the messages should provide relevant and valuable information that potential real estate buyers and sellers need to know. That way, you can continue earning their trust.

- Update your blog – Ensure that you constantly update your professional blog. It contributes to building and maintaining your relationship with your prospects. However, avoid posting blogs that are exclusively sales-oriented because such a theme is already what your actual real estate agent website is focusing on.

  In your blog, talk about in-home family activity recommendations, market updates, and how-to articles. Provide checklists on home cleaning and maintenance, too. Your goal here is to let your prospects know that you are indeed a great source of information on the topic, which is a great way to entice them to keep coming back. You could also add packing and moving tips.

- Take advantage of the power of social media – You can also continue communicating with your prospects through your social media accounts. Among the best social networks that you can use for communication would be Facebook, Instagram, LinkedIn, and Twitter.

When communicating through the above-mentioned channels, do not forget to include links to valuable and informative articles and updates. Set a goal to keep your prospects informed and occupied. Ensure that you also re-share and like the interesting and vital updates they have on their pages too.

- Organize relevant events – If you have the resources and capability, you may also want to host a weekly or monthly gathering where you will be available to respond questions related to real estate that your prospects may want to ask. Make sure to do it in an informal and relaxed environment.

When choosing the place to conduct the event or gathering, think of the things you love and enjoy the most. Ask yourself where you often spend a lot of your time, too. It could be a gym or any other relaxing location. Find out whether you can rent a space or room for just an hour or so in such a location. You may want to hold your get-together there, as it allows you to communicate with your audience without feeling too flustered.

- Create a monthly newsletter – Remember that aggressive emailing and cold calling are effective prospecting techniques, particularly if the people you are reaching out to are really ready to sell or buy a home. The problem is that you can't expect all your prospects to be at that stage. With that said, you need to do something to stay in touch with your prospects without looking too pushy.

An effective technique is to send newsletters and make it a monthly thing. Sending a monthly newsletter to your prospects is a powerful way of showing them that you are thinking about them. Do not forget to incorporate real estate information and valuable market statistics in your newsletters. Include the latest news, happenings, and notes in the specific area where you are specializing in.

Apply these tips so you can always make your prospects feel like they are truly important to you. Remember that staying in touch with them can help you achieve success when prospecting and closing real estate deals, so do something to interact and communicate with them regularly.

How to Generate Referrals and Build Your Referral Base

As a real estate agent, you are probably aware that referrals are your ultimate sources of new business and leads. The problem is that a lot of agents still struggle with consistently getting such referrals. The good news is that once you get referrals and prospects through this route, most of the work is often already done.

The reason is that you have already established trust since you were recommended by happy and satisfied clients. With that said, it is safe to say that referrals are truly capable of building your credibility and trustworthiness – both of which are strong foundations for effective selling. So how can you generate referrals? These tips can help:

Make Sure You Are Referable

To ensure that referral marketing will turn out to be a proactive and valuable part of your effort toward generating leads when prospecting, you have to work on becoming a referable agent. You can do that by earning the trust of your clients. Work on delivering what you promise and do it within the promised timeline. Your past and present clients should be able to speak about the value of your offered services.

Avoid Relying on Accidental Referrals

Another important tip when trying to generate referrals and create a solid referral base is to avoid depending too much on accidental referrals. This means that you have to be extremely clear as to the specific clients you want to target. You also have to clarify the exact manner through which your network can help you generate such referrals from your clients.

Never Let Your Pipeline Get Dry

You have to set up an effective sales referral process at the beginning of your career to prevent your pipeline from running dry. Note that your success as a real estate agent and in prospecting will be even more achievable if you can attract consistently high-quality referrals. This will lower your risk of being left scrambling once your pipeline stops flowing.

One great tip is to create a referral program that has complementary providers so you can exchange referrals. Just make sure that the providers included in the program or network are the ones you can comfortably and confidently refer or recommend to your best clients and friends or relatives.

Do Not Forget to Thank the Sources of Your Referrals

Apart from generating referrals and solidifying your referral base, this tip also works to expand your relationship with your referrals and their sources. You have to recognize their support and effort to refer you to the people close to them.

You can do that by sending them a message showing your gratitude. It could be a simple handwritten note, an email, or a phone call. Your goal here is to express your gratitude and appreciation for their help. Doing this is also good for you as it can further result in garnering additional referrals.

Look For Other Ways through Which Your Clients Can Recommend You

If your clients are incapable of referring you directly to the people they know, you should be able to provide them with other techniques that will let them recommend you. That way, they can choose a method that they can confidently and comfortably use. For instance, you may ask them to provide testimonials on any platform after working with you.

Inform Your Clients about All Your Offered Products and Services

By doing that, the clients who were satisfied with your offers in the past will know exactly what to say when referring you to the people they know. Avoid assuming that your clients already know everything about what you do.

Inform them about the different forms of assistance and help you can offer in the real estate market. That way, they can immediately recommend you in case someone in their circle is seeking those services.

Do not forget to show how remarkable your company is by reminding your clients of the reasons that make your company different. Ensure that they will always have something positive to say to their network, resulting in more referrals that will turn into actual clients.

Maintain Excellent Relationships with Clients and Prospects

After working successfully with a client, focus on strengthening your relationship with them. Make sure that it continues for a long time, too. For instance, you may want to send your clients valuable and helpful content, such as homeowner tips or any relevant information that will help them, even if you have already completed your transaction.

You should take the time and effort to remain helpful to your clients even after closing a sale. By doing that, you can establish trust, which is a big help if you want them to be reminded of you and your services in case someone from their circle needs it.

Also, remember that although a lead is not yet officially interested in doing business with you, you should never abandon the connection and relationship completely. Note that there is still a chance for this lead to turn into your client in the future or possibly become just another great source of referrals. You have to be open to possibilities, so make sure that you stay in touch and send constant follow-ups.

Establish Relationships and Connections with Industry Leaders

Prospecting and gaining referrals also involves building relationships with renowned leaders in the real estate industry. These include professionals in selling and buying homes, like housing inspectors, brokers, mortgage lenders, and construction companies.

If you work together and strengthen your relationship and trust with other industry leaders and professionals, cross-promoting each other's services while significantly increasing your referrals is a great possibility. What is great about it is that it can make the process of buying and selling a home even smoother and quicker.

One way to build this kind of relationship is to attend trade shows and networking events in the industry frequently. You also have to strengthen your social media presence. Those techniques can help to build your network through various means, which can also help to increase your referrals eventually.

Focus on strengthening relationships as the stronger these are, the higher your chances of gaining referrals. It can make you a popular and recognizable real estate agent, which can contribute a lot to getting new leads.

Chapter 4
Winning the Deal

Winning a deal will always be the ultimate goal of most real estate agents. The question is, how should you do it? As a beginner, you may still be confused about how you should win and close deals with your leads and prospects. Fortunately, most of the things you need to know about winning and closing deals are included in this chapter. With the information here, you will receive guidance throughout the process of communicating with your prospects.

Making Your Listing Presentation a Masterpiece

As a real estate agent, you are already probably aware of how important your listing presentation is when it comes to winning deals. A listing presentation refers to the pitch you should deliver to a potential seller. It indicates how you plan to represent them in real estate transactions.

A great listing presentation can provide data about the local market. It should also provide comparable sales. It needs to offer insight into your marketing strategies for the prospect's home. Moreover, there should be social proof that you are indeed a top-notch real estate agent.

If you succeed with the presentation, then it can lead to signing on a new client, which can also result in receiving a higher commission for the month. However, you need to make your listing presentation as impressive as possible, so you won't end up getting rejected. In that case, here are a few components of your listing presentation that you should focus on if you want to leave a positive impression.

Lead/Brief Intro

Open up the presentation with the lead or brief intro. Note, though, that the most successful listing presentations are often those that begin with only a quick overview. It should only involve a recap of who you are, your success record, the specific things you do, and the services you offer.

Note that your prospects want to gain a hundred percent assurance about your ability to close the deal within their preferred timeframe. The faster you close the deal at a profitable price, the better. With that in mind, you need to show them some data and examples that serve as proof of your skills and abilities in this area.

During the first few slides of your presentation, you should be able to provide brief yet concise information about your top skills, the number of houses you have successfully sold around the area or neighborhood recently, together with the types of property sold, particularly a property that is similar to the type owned by your prospects.

The intro should also present important figures from your previous deals and transactions. It could be a comparison of the original price used for listing the property and the final amount you have successfully closed with your previous buyers. Just make sure that the last figure is higher than the former. Include how many days, on average, the property appears on the market before you close a sale, too. All these details will validate your higher rate of commission.

Wrap up this opening by letting your prospect know what to expect during the remaining parts of the listing presentation. Indicate the points you will be talking about and how long the talk will probably take. Assure your prospect that they are allowed to ask questions during your talk.

Give your prospects such information upfront as it can help them to focus on the things you have to say. It will also let them anticipate what will come next, thereby making them more focused throughout the process. It can even motivate them during the talk.

Setup

The first component of your listing presentation has probably enlightened your prospect about your intentions and what they should expect from you. Once you achieve that, you can move on to the next component, which is the setup. To make the setup component impressive, take advantage of all the extensive research you did beforehand. You can do that by showing your prospect that you are fully knowledgeable, not only about the property but also about the neighborhood and community.

Reassure your prospect that you are aware of what the market can expect to receive from that particular home. Make the setup component a masterpiece by ensuring that it clearly paints a picture of the present conditions in the market. It should provide proof that now is the perfect time to sell the home. Aside from that, let your prospect know that you are indeed knowledgeable about everything related to the market as well as the key factors that can impact the sale.

One indication that you have constructed this component well is if it ends up letting your prospect know if the actual results achieved were as you predicted. It should also relay to them what your expectations are regarding the possible performance of the property, provided it is appropriately priced and listed.

When creating this section, remember that it is usually the part where the prospect will start losing interest. Bearing that in mind, ensure that you hit all the high and positive points. Answer their questions promptly, if there are any, too. Keep in mind that you need to be persuasive during the presentation, so ensure that the narrative keeps moving. Your goal here is to convince them that they should list their properties with you.

Delivery

This is another vital component of the listing presentation, which should come right after the setup. Unlike the setup that focuses on convincing your prospect of the benefits of selling their home and asking for your help with it, the delivery section is all about providing answers on how you should do it. It is where you have to lay out your exact plan.

You will be providing your prospect with information on how you intend to get their property onto the market, put it in front of appropriate buyers at the perfect time, make it relevant even with numerous other properties sprouting (competitors), and sell it at the best possible price.

Be very clear when it comes to laying out your plan. Your goal here should be to end the section with your prospects being completely aware of the high-level techniques you intend to use to market and sell their property successfully.

Question and Answer

This is the time when you allow your prospect to ask questions. Sure, they may have asked you a few questions during the first few parts of your presentation, but in this specific part, expect to be bombarded with a lot of additional questions.

As much as possible, try to convince your prospects to hold whatever questions they have in mind and ask them at the end so you can deliver an effective presentation of what you offer. That way, you may have already shown your extensive knowledge on the subject and market and have laid out how you plan to market the property. In that case, you are already prepared to answer questions.

During this specific part of your presentation, ask your clients about the specific areas where they think they need more clarification. Request their feedback, too. Consider this specific part of the listing presentation as the time to get your prospects completely involved in the conversation.

Make them feel like they are truly part of the whole process. By doing that, you can increase your chances of convincing them to collaborate and work with you when it comes to marketing and selling their property.

Also, make sure that you observe their reactions closely throughout the first three parts of your presentation – the lead, setup, and delivery. Have you noticed them pausing at certain portions of your presentation? Take note of those instances and sections when you felt like your prospects were hesitating. Solicit questions and feedback from those sections first.

Close

The close serves as the last part of the presentation. It is the shortest, so expect to have an easier time memorizing it. However, remember that it is also the most crucial part of your presentation, which makes it somewhat nerve-wracking to deliver. It is the exact moment when you ask the prospect to sign up with your agency.

Expect them to waffle back and forth to decide; this may take a few days. They will think about whether it is a great idea to seek your help or use another listing agent. They may even start to have second thoughts about whether to list the home at all.

The whole process may be tedious and frustrating not only for you but also for your prospects. Because of that, it would be best to give them the chance to do whatever they intend to do initially. If possible, ask them for a specific answer as to whether or not they want to work with you.

Additional Tips in Making Your Listing Presentation More Attractive

Apart from putting your focus on crafting the previously discussed components of your listing presentation, you can also make the final output more attractive with these simple yet powerful tips:

- Avoid talking too much about yourself – Yes, you may be tempted to talk extensively about your successes and impressive career, so you can convince your prospects that you are the perfect agent for them. However, it's not a good idea to focus too much on yourself.

  Focus more on the goals of your prospects and reflect on how you can offer your help. Keep in mind that the other agents will also brag about the marketing techniques they have in store for their prospects. Try to act differently by being the trusted advisor capable of putting the concerns and goals of your clients first before commissions.

- Incorporate plenty of visuals in the presentation – Note that the economic and social challenges at present may prompt your prospects to bombard you with questions. With that in mind, you should prepare yourself to answer such questions and something to make all nuances, complexities, and jargon in your presentation easy to grasp and comprehend. This makes it necessary to incorporate visuals.

Apart from making your presentation more appealing, adding visuals can also make it more persuasive. Incorporate relevant images, infographics, charts, and graphs in your presentation. All these visuals can help you to effectively communicate even the more complex topics about the real estate industry.

- Do not overload your prospects with data – In relation to the adding of visuals, avoid overdoing it to the point that your presentation becomes overloaded with data. You don't want to confuse your prospects even more by showing them too many slides of irrelevant graphs and charts.

Focus on the key details and try to simplify those concepts that you think they can't grasp that easily. Make the design of your listing presentation stand out but avoid overloading it with too many visuals. If possible, apply an infographic design. It can contribute a lot in visualizing your data, pulling out the most important figures, and engaging your prospects.

- Add animations effectively – If you are using PowerPoint for your presentation, which is what most, if not all, agents use, you can access a huge collection of ready-to-use animations. You may also want to create your own by taking advantage of custom animations.

  Use these animations the right way as they can help to break up the data in your slides, which is a powerful way of delivering your message more effectively. Just remember that simplicity is still the key. Sometimes, the only thing you need is a wipe animation or subtle fade. It will be enough to add life to your presentation.

- Make your presentation interactive – You do not have to present your listing presentation in a fully linear way. Make it more intuitive and interactive by adding hyperlinks throughout your slides. By doing that, your presentation will become more receptive to the responses of your audience or prospects. You may also want to use SMS Polls, which refers to a tool that lets you interact with your audience through surveys and live polls.

In addition to the tips above, make sure to constantly update yourself on the latest trends when it comes to delivering listing presentations. Your goal should be to add these trends to your own presentation, so it will turn out to be exciting and fresh. Just don't forget its key and salient points. Remember your ultimate goal, and that is to convince your target audience that you are indeed the right person for the job.

Qualifying your Listing Prospects

Qualifying your leads or listing prospects is also a vital part of trying to win deals. Basically, it involves a systematic process where you will gather details about your prospects and leads so you can scrutinize whether they are capable, ready, and eager to either buy or sell. This stage often happens early in the pipeline or sales funnel, usually during your initial contact.

If your goal is to succeed as a real estate agent, then set your own criteria when it comes to qualifying leads and prospects. This will allow you to disqualify those who do not meet your criteria. While you may feel bad about the disqualification process at first, remind yourself that it is extremely important as it will let you focus more on promising leads and prospects.

So how can you qualify listing prospects? You may use the following factors that many successful real estate agents now use to accurately qualify leads, accelerate the sales cycle, and close more deals.

Location

You have to consider your target location when it comes to qualifying leads. For instance, if you work as an agent in Chicago, then you will never target buyers who are looking for property in Minneapolis. They are irrelevant leads and may only be time-wasters since you can't offer your services to them even if they are qualified based on other factors.

Ideally, you need to look for leads who are searching for properties in the specific market you are focusing on. This will allow you to show your knowledge and expertise in the market more efficiently. You can also present a list of the most suitable properties that your leads and prospects may like.

To ensure that your leads/prospects are qualified based on the location factor, try to gather the following information the first time you communicate with them:

• The exact property they want

• Zip code of the area/neighborhood they prefer

• Whether they are open to view the same properties in other areas/neighborhoods

• Whether they are open to checking out properties in a town or city that is nearby

Aside from those details, find out how knowledgeable they are about the housing market, too. Determining their level of knowledge on real estate business and the market as such will give you an idea of whether they have also done their research.

Remember that there are instances when you also need to work with knowledgeable and educated leads. If they are knowledgeable, then there is a high likelihood of them wanting to push the transaction through right away. This can result in a smoother and quicker lead conversion process.

Reason/Motivation for Buying or Selling

Another crucial factor that should help you to qualify leads or prospects is the actual reason or motivation for buying or selling. You have to identify their actual reason for reaching out to real estate agents like you. Some potential reasons why they reach out to you may be that it is their first time buying or selling a home and their intention to downsize or move up. It could also be due to their retirement, a sudden change in a job, or a plan to invest in real estate.

Identify the exact reason for contacting you as this will let you know whether they are motivated enough for you to convert them into actual paying clients. You can also use the identified reason or motivation to find the property that is an ideal match for the client based on their exact needs and wants. Using that, you can guide them into an actual home purchase or win the deal with them with their guaranteed satisfaction.

Budget/Price Point

You can also qualify listing prospects and leads based on the budget or price point. If you are dealing with someone who plans to buy a home, find out how much they are willing and can afford to spend. Your prospect's budget is a key factor in deciding whether they are qualified. The reason is that it can help you determine right away if they can afford to continue with the transaction and make the actual purchase of the property.

If they can, then both parties are heading in the right direction. Note, however, that there are prospects who have no idea if they can afford their preferred property. In that case, you can be of help by inquiring about the following:

- How much did they set aside for the down payment?

- Is their credit score good enough?

- Do they have existing debts? If there is, how much?

The answers to such questions are essential as those can impact the amount your prospects will most likely spend on the actual property. It can also answer your question as to whether your prospects are already pre-approved by certain lenders.

These factors are important because they affect how much your real estate leads can afford to buy and whether they'll get pre-approved by a lender. If they're willing to provide this type of information and make changes, they may still be qualified leads.

Your prospect's actual budget can also help you to narrow down your list of properties. It prevents you from wasting time looking for and introducing properties to your prospects and leads that go beyond their budget or price point.

Other Agents, They May Have Been Working With

Another crucial factor that will help you decide whether to qualify leads or prospects is whether or not they are also working with other agents. Note that many leads tend to work with a couple of agents simultaneously. They may have different reasons for doing so – one of which is that they are unhappy and unsatisfied with the service of the first agent.

Of course, you need to find out first whether this is the case with your leads before delivering your presentation to them. This is to lower the risk of you dealing with a prospect or lead who may cancel your service at any time.

However, avoid directly asking your prospects if they are already working with an agent. The reason is that they may not tell you about it honestly since they are still be hoping to hear your offer. One effective way to phrase the question is to ask about the various tactics your prospects have already used in their search for homes.

You may receive a more candid answer if you deliver the question in that way. With that information, you can decide based on their answers whether the leads or prospects are qualified and worth your time. If their answers signify that they have already contacted other agents apart from you, then you may want to ask why they have contacted you too.

If they say that their reason is dissatisfaction or that it is already the end of their contract or agreement, then you may want to push through with your presentation. Just make sure that you spend time investigating even further how you can be of help. In case you are the only agent they are currently communicating with, then you may continue by directly assessing how qualified your prospects are based on other relevant factors.

Timeline

This factor answers the length of time your prospects intend to wait to sell their property or buy a new home. Note that successful agents in the industry are aware of the length of the sales cycle taken from the first contact with the prospect to the close or end of the transaction.

By asking them their preferred or targeted timeline, you can also identify what specific part of your real estate sales funnel or cycle your lead is presently in. With this relevant detail, you can create your sales technique accordingly.

Ensure that you get precise answers in this area. Keep in mind that their preciseness is also an indication of their willingness to act now, making them qualified leads. You may also want to ask them about the following as the answers will help you figure out the exact timeline:

- How long have they been looking for a home?
- Are they still waiting to sell their current home before purchasing a new one?
- Are they fully prepared to buy a house and move anytime soon?
- Can they move right away in case you find the perfect home for them within just a couple of days?

The details you can gather from the previous questions will help you figure out whether your prospects have realistic timelines. For instance, if their timelines are still in the next two to three years, then it is possible that they will not turn into actual leads in the long run. Your goal here is to find prospective clients who have urgent reasons to buy or sell a property as they are the ones with a higher conversion rate.

In addition to the factors already mentioned, it also helps to keep the following tips in mind when qualifying leads or prospects:

- Take advantage of automation tools – Set your lead qualification system on autopilot as doing so will improve its efficiency, which can also result in higher revenue. You should be able to gather all the needed demographic data on your prospects and leads, such as financing and budget. You can make that possible with automation tools.

- Create a lead profile and scoring system – Ensure that you have already developed the perfect customer profile prior to communicating with and contacting leads. Your goal here is to just identify the things that make a buyer or seller perfect. The profile should also indicate the specific clients you wish to work with, especially when it comes to demographics, priorities, needs, values, and research habits.

  Having a detailed customer or client profile before generating and qualifying real estate leads will prevent you from wasting time on unnecessary things. Once you already have the profile set in place, you can provide every lead with a score depending on the level of their suitability to the customer profile.

For instance, score them based on their level of qualifications as well as their exact position in the real estate pipeline or sales funnel.

- Prepare extensively before contacting prospects – Regardless of whether you will be contacting your leads or prospects online or you have acquired them from referrals or your previous clients, it is still necessary to be fully prepared.

Develop a concrete plan on how you should carry the conversation. This does not necessarily mean following and sticking with a script. Still, it helps to prepare a list of relevant questions, so you can easily insert them smoothly into your conversations.

Avoid quickly bombarding your prospects with questions to the point that they may feel like you are actually interrogating them. Also, ensure that you are not the only one who talks. You also have to let your prospects talk and listen to them intently.

Make sure that your conversation is fun and engaging, too. By doing that, you can determine their actual motivations while giving you the chance to approach them professionally. This move can also contribute a lot toward effectively detecting your most qualified leads.

- Avoid giving up on certain leads too quickly - Never assume that just because a lead or prospect is not fully prepared yet, he/she is already a dead-end lead. While it is important to prioritize the qualified ones, you should never neglect the other prospects and leads who are part of your pipeline.

Instead of completely ignoring and forgetting them, include them in a lead nurturing campaign. Remember that even those who have no clear timeline yet may turn into your best clients once they are already prepared to buy or sell. To ensure that you will not miss that opportunity, you may want to just provide them with updates on the housing market every now and then.

Send monthly newsletters to them, too. In addition, you should try contacting them in the next couple of years to follow up about their plans. Your goal here is to build a strong relationship with them until the time when they are already prepared to buy.

By doing that, combined with the use of advanced and automated tools and strategies as well as the lead profile, you will have an easier time isolating hot leads and nurturing the cold ones. This can give you a much better chance of reaching your goal soon.

Once you already have a list of your qualified prospects, it is time to present to them. You can deliver your presentation to such qualified prospects by just sticking to these very simple tips and tricks:

Utilize a Distinctive Value Proposition

It should serve as your elevator pitch, which does not only help to qualify sales prospects but give them a clear idea about exactly what you do. This proposition should contain a power statement or two. It should be something that they want and can easily and quickly grasp. You can present it as just one sentence or paragraph. Some even present their value proposition within just a few words, provided they are unique and can truly grab the attention of their target leads.

Focus On a Measurable Business Objective

When delivering your presentation, ensure that your focus sticks to a measurable business goal. It can contribute to capturing their attention and interest. You can effectively gain their interest, especially if the metric you are focusing on has a great impact on the overall results.

Show How It Can Disrupt the Status Quo

You are probably already aware of how powerful the status quo is. Most people are not even in favor of change. You can only expect them to veer away from the norm or the status quo when they feel like doing so can dramatically improve their present situation. It should be that their move can increase their sales, improve their efficiency, reduce cost, or lessen their stress. Your presentation should be able to show that you are capable of doing that for them.

Provide Evidence or Proof

You also need to show your target audience that you are indeed a great real estate agent. In that case, it helps to provide valuable and credible information about your huge contributions to your past clients who have similar situations to your present prospects. By showing proof of your ability to help, you can instantly show your credibility in the industry.

Dealing with Sales Objections

For you to attain success as a real estate agent, you have to be fully prepared to deal with a lot of sales objections. Note that these objections may happen anytime during your presentation or whenever you try to win a deal.

Aside from objections, expect several questions to be thrown at you during the time when you are still delivering your presentation. It is natural, though, considering the fact that your leads are still trying to get to know you.

Still, you don't have to fret as each question or every objection your leads or prospects may raise serves as a chance for you to prove your skills and expertise. You should look at it as an opportunity to establish trust, too. Just make sure that you are completely prepared so you can answer their questions or counter their objections.

Among the questions that your leads and prospects may ask that will most likely lead to them rejecting your service if they are unsatisfied with your answers are:

• How do you perceive your agency compared to the others?

• What are your designations, certifications, and qualifications?

- How can you prove that you are indeed trustworthy?

- Can you share specific details regarding your previous real estate transactions?

Remember that some questions are quite hard to anticipate, so it is necessary to be prepared for everything. As for the actual objections, one of the statements you may hear will question your fee, and you should be prepared for it.

"Is it okay with you to lower your commission?"

Once you deal with a client who draws the "lower your commission card," you may naturally be tempted to prove your worth. You may do that by starting to explain the things that you can do as well as the specific reasons why you are worth the indicated commission. The problem is that your prospects and leads may view such reasoning as excuses.

Rather than responding to this objection by turning the entire conversation into a sort of self-presentation, your response should focus more on your prospect. This means that you should let them know how important it is for you to have that commission so you can also give them what they want in return. Show them that working with you can actually help them achieve their main goal of saving money.

"Some agents will offer their services for less."

When a prospect objects using this statement, take note that it is often just a trick. The truth is that in most cases, they have no intention of working with other agents. Some prospects think that whenever they deliver this objection, the real estate agent will automatically lower the rate to prevent them from going elsewhere.

The reason is that most of them look at real estate agents as some kind of service they can get in other places for a lower cost. To deal with this objection, try reframing this common mindset of your prospects. What you should do is to prove to them that you are not just a mere service. You are actually an opportunity worth paying the right amount to.

"I would like to sell the property myself."

If you receive this objection, then it is highly likely that the prospect underestimates the kind and amount of work delivered by real estate agents when it comes to selling a house. It could be that they have learned about the entire process online and felt like it is not that hard. It could also be that they had a bad experience with another agent before.

Regardless of what made them think that your job is easy, you should try uncovering gently the specific reason why they prefer selling their property without any help. Once you get to the bottom of it, you can then encourage them by explaining they will actually enjoy more benefits when they decide to work with an agent because it frees up their time to prepare for a move.

You may also want to follow this objection with a question so you can encourage them to be more specific as to their reasons.

"I am not sure if I'm ready."

Just like when you hear some objections saying the properties are not on the market, you should also try to detect the reasons why your prospects are not ready to sell or buy a property yet. For instance, they may not be ready because they have a feeling that they will be able to sell their property for a higher amount in the future.

If that is their reason, then show them how you intend to offer greater value to their property even if it is sold now. You should show them such value even before the start of the selling process. By doing that, your prospects will not feel like they are forced to commit even if they are not fully prepared for it. The other thing to bear in mind is that if they sell later, they will also pay more for a property if the market does rise.

"I'm not interested."

In most cases, this objection is often directed to agents, not the actual transaction. When that happens, pinpoint the exact reason why they do not like working with agents. After uncovering the reason, you should enlighten them by directly addressing it in your presentation or pitch.

Also, try to prove your worth, but maybe not during the actual presentation, to prevent making your prospects feel that you are forcing yourself on them. You can do it by staying in touch with them more consistently compared to other real estate agents in the neighborhood. Just make sure that you also have the best sales platform, one that promotes ease by keeping in touch with your prospects.

Those are just many of the potential objections you may hear. The best way to handle such objections is to always see each one as an opportunity or possibility. Address the core objections of your leads or prospects and try to prove your value, albeit subtly. By doing that, you can build and take advantage of an opportunity in areas where other real estate agents have failed.

Asking for the Business

Once you have completed your listing presentation, you may be wondering what you should do next to increase your chances of winning the business. You are probably hoping that you will head back to the office and schedule an appointment with a photographer, so you can start taking pictures of the new listing. By this time, you may have already accomplished all of the following:

- Acquired all the important information about the property – You may even have taken a look at the premises already.
- Asked questions and responded to their concerns, needs, and questions
- Shown how certain services you offer can address their exact concerns and needs
- Discussed and reached a consensus on the listing price

During your presentation, though, it is crucial to withhold the talk about the final listing price at the time when you are already nearing the stage of asking for the business. Yes, you need to come to your appointment prepared with a price range. However, you also need to consider all the information you gathered after asking questions and discussing things on the spot.

With that information, you can reach a final recommendation that is comfortable for you. Therefore, withhold talking about the price until all your questions, and those of your prospects, are answered. Now that you have reached this far, probably the only thing that is left for you to ask is whether they want to list their property with you. Ask them directly.

Regardless of the response of your prospects, do not forget to say thank you. Thank your prospects and leads for the time they dedicated to hearing your presentation. Aside from it showing that you have good manners, it also means good business. By saying a simple "thank you," you are showing them that you value the time and opportunity, they offered to you so you could discuss business. You can also use it as a convenient point for follow-up contacts.

The question is, how can you deliver your "thank you" effectively? Try going for something non-confrontational. It could be in the form of a letter or postcard. However, remember that this indirect communication has a low chance of keeping your communications and conversation going. It would be better to send a text message or a phone call instead.

Bringing the Presentation to a Conclusion

How can you conclude your listing presentation? To be a successful real estate agent, you should have your own way of ending your presentations in such a way that it will remind your prospects that you are the best person to help them. Even if they tell you that they will still need time to think about your offer, you should still end up your presentation pleasantly.

Your goal is to ensure that you leave a good impression, so you will always be in their minds at the time when they finally decide to use the services of an agent. The best way for you to wrap up the presentation is to provide a killer case study. It serves as social proof that also directly illustrates your professional skills and expertise.

Avoid making this conclusion lengthy, though. A wise tip is to stick to a simple formula for copywriting. An example of the formula you can use would be:

- Client background – middle-aged couple based in New York
- Challenge – the problem/s faced by those past clients – It could be that they had to sell their house within just a month in an area or neighborhood that is not so popular.
- Solution – the exact technique used by you and your agency to help the couple
- Results – quick figures illustrating the positive outcome after they sought your help (ex. sold the house in just 3 weeks at a cost that is 5% higher than the first listing price)

By providing them with this case study that demonstrates how good you are, you can end your listing presentation on a positive note. It can even help motivate your prospects or leads to take action, which will end up with you winning the deal.

Chapter 5

Getting the Home Ready for a Showing

After successfully winning the deal, expect the real work to begin. Now, you should start all the necessary preparations to get the home ready for the actual showing. This is where you will get really busy, but you can simplify the entire process by collaborating with the homeowner as well as the company you are working for. You can also take a look at this chapter as it will guide you throughout the process of preparing the home for a showing.

Getting the Home Ready for Pictures and Virtual Tour

Before the actual showing, it would be ideal to prepare the home for pictures and a virtual tour. Note that nowadays, real estate agents and sellers have the chance to provide prospective buyers with an interactive online/virtual experience guaranteed to be truly immersive, especially if you also combine it with high-quality pictures.

The good news is that preparing this virtual tour is not that hard or expensive. As a matter of fact, you won't spend a lot on this marketing technique at all. Most virtual house tour options, like video chat tours and 3D walkthroughs, even let prospective buyers interact with real estate agents while exploring every bit of the house. It would be like you are letting the potential buyer tour in person. With that, you can use this technique to attract homebuyers regardless of where they are.

However, you have to know exactly how to stand out from the sea of competitors. Here are the things you should focus on if you want to make the virtual tour more engaging and attractive to a lot of buyers, instead of just being a simple slideshow or listing video:

- Actual view of the home – It should not just be a rendering or recreation.
- Smooth navigation, promoting ease in moving from one room to another – It should pan 360 degrees, too.
- A feature that allows viewers to go back, walkthrough, or freeze the screen or frame
- High-definition and clear pictures
- Clutter-free shots and images
- Emphasize the best features of the house – These should include outdoor spaces and unique facilities and amenities.
- Pictures captured from the greatest vantage point – Each picture should clearly show the room or a specific area of the house in its entirety.
- Compatibility with different devices – The tour should be viewable regardless of the mobile device used by the buyer.

If you are planning to shoot the virtual tour on your own, then make sure that you already set a plan in place. Determine the best viewpoints and angles you should include in the tour. One of the most important tips during this stage is to test out various angles so you can determine the specific vantage points capable of showing the best features of the home.

Test the height of the camera, too, as this will let you determine how it can change or alter the lighting. Another thing that you should do when preparing for the virtual tour of the house on your own is to print out the floor plan if it is available. Alternatively, you can put tape on the floor. This should serve as your marker as to where you should stand for every shot.

Even if shooting the video for the virtual tour may sound simple, note that the 3D tour is much more complex and requires additional forethought. With that, you also need to complete the following tasks before the actual day you intend to record the tour:

- Complete all the necessary updates – Similar to when taking professional still images, ensure that you have also completed all pre-listing updates that you think are necessary before recording the video. These include cleaning, painting, and landscaping. Note that the virtual tour will also serve as a viewing, so you need to make the home look at its best.

- Complete the staging – If you have plans to stage the home with new furnishings and décor, then complete it prior to the virtual tour. As much as possible, declutter the home. You also need to remove all excess items from the site, so you can clearly show the property's best features.

- Do the shoot a couple of days before the actual listing – Schedule the capture of the virtual tour at almost the same time you take professional pictures. Doing so will save you a lot of time for preparation. This will allow you to do the cleaning, decluttering, and staging just once. Apart from that, you have an assurance that all marketing materials feature a consistent feel and look.

During the day of the shooting, make sure that the house is already free of clutter. You should have also solved the problem with poor lighting. This means that you have already determined where you should take a shot to enhance the lighting.

While the majority of the preparation work may have already been completed before the shoot, you should still perform the following task on an actual day:
- Do a quick cleanup and polishing.
- Remove all unnecessary items you do not want to show in the virtual tour – These include trash cans and cleaning supplies.
- Open the blinds and turn all the lights on.

- Open all doors inside the house – This will prevent any interruption when navigating from one room to another.
- Wipe the lens of the camera – This can assure you that all the captured pictures will be totally clear.
- Reshoot areas that you captured when your camera was unsteady – Do the same when the transition from one room to another looks choppy.

The ultimate goal should always be bringing out the best of the home during the virtual tour. Apart from preparing for the virtual tour, focus on having professional pictures taken. Note that the listing images are the first things that prospective buyers will see. Pictures will help them decide whether they should ask for the virtual tour.

If possible, seek the help of professional photographers as they know the proper lighting and angles when shooting pictures. They can also see even the tiniest details that can depict the home better. Moreover, they can help to capture the selling points of the home, which can further increase its chance of getting sold fast.

Counseling Clients on Home Improvements

Advising your clients on the necessary home improvements should also form part of the tasks you need to do before the actual showing of the home. You need to counsel your clients on what they should do to make their home for sale fully prepared for that moment. If you notice a problem that you think affects the physical features of the house, inform the client right away. That way, they can make the necessary improvements before you actually show the property to potential buyers.

Basically, the major improvements that can have a positive impact on the final price of the property will be those that can bring it back to a good standard, correct its defects, and improve its first impressions or curb appeal. For instance, if a home you are preparing shows has horribly dated decoration, you may want to advise your clients to add some modern touches to the interiors. That way, the design will be aligned to what most present buyers expect.

Ensure that your suggestions do not make your clients go overboard with improvements, though. The only things that they need to do is install a more modern and reasonable color scheme or updating the interiors in such a way that buyers will feel like they can move into the house right away without undertaking major facelifts. Some great pieces of advice that you can offer your clients for home improvements would be:

- Keep it simple – Note that a complete overhaul or redecoration is not advisable. It is unnecessary. You should just aim to get the house into a reasonably current and acceptable color scheme as far as the paint, floor coverings, and counters are concerned.

- Avoid creating a design showpiece – Remind your clients that the actual buyers will usually do significant alterations to the home so they can call it their own. As the seller, only aim to improve the home in such a way that the buyers will not feel like the alterations they intend to do should be immediate. They should be able to do it at a later time.

- Prioritize the big stuff – It could be making the interiors of the home appear current and properly maintaining the yard, patios, decks, and landscaping. It can make the buyers feel like the responsibility to make huge changes in the property is not immediate. This will encourage them to invest in the home. You can expect them to present a more competitive offer initially than when the house you have presented comes with major repair and interior/exterior color issues.

- Repaint – Note that even just a bit of repainting can create a major impact on the home. Ask your client to repaint the home, if necessary, as it is a cost-effective method of freshening the property up. It can even help to disguise some of the shortcomings in the design of the home.

Apart from the previous tips, you should also counsel your clients to correct any major defects. Advise them to veer away from the most recent trends. Instead of following the recent trend of using deep colors on walls, recommend the use of a blank and warm canvas instead. That way, the prospective buyer will feel like they can easily work with it to make it their own if they decide to buy the house.

Passing the Curb Appeal Test

As the real estate agent hired by your clients, you should also exert an effort to help them supercharge the curb appeal of their properties. The curb appeal is extremely important as it can significantly improve the way a home looks to a potential buyer. It includes everything about the house, including the exteriors, driveway, front yard, paint job, patio, the front door, and the interiors.

Advise your clients to improve the curb appeal of the home. The reason is that all cost-effective improvements that contribute to the home's curb appeal can significantly increase the selling price. The good news is that your client does not have to spend a huge sum of money to boost their property's curb appeal. As a matter of fact, beautifying the front exterior is actually inexpensive. Just make sure that you and your client are willing to do a bit of work.

Among the tips that can help the home pass the curb appeal test and improve it without requiring your client to spend a lot would be:

- Strategic landscaping – Remember that the exterior of the home is the first thing that prospective buyers will see. This is true whether they drive through the neighborhood or browse through the listings. Bearing that in mind, focus on strategic landscaping that can help improve the looks of the home without the need for costly remodeling. Work together with your client to make the grounds of their property look as good as possible. It can significantly improve the home's curb appeal without costing too much.

- Do a thorough cleaning – In this case, pressure washing the home can be the ultimate solution. It can contribute a lot toward removing the grime, moss, and dirt that may have built up for years. Through this approach, you no longer have to replace exterior tiles and bricks. There is also no need to repaint the whole home, which can only be an added expense for your client.

- Do some touch-ups – After pressure washing, you can expect the house to be in pristine condition once again. In that case, repainting may no longer be necessary. Just a simple trim and touch-up on the front door can help. You may also want to advise your client to brighten the façade by adding a touch of contrasting shades or colors. Even a simple pop of color can already help to freshen up the place.

- Check the mailbox – If the mailbox is installed on the street, then it is highly likely that it is already slightly beaten up. If it is attached to the house, then the owner may have already neglected it as far as its aesthetics is concerned. It is time to give the mailbox some attention.

Have it painted, polished, or replaced. Believe me, it can contribute a lot to boosting the home's curb appeal.

- Clean and repair the roof – Check the house's roofing fixtures. Are there loose singles or any other visible roof damage? Then inform the homeowner to have those things fixed before the actual showing of the house.

  In case the roof is still new and in excellent condition, there is still some work needed – and that involves cleaning all leaves, pine needles, spare pickleball, and any other debris that accumulated there. Note that a lot of buyers are picky when it comes to the roofing condition, so examine it beforehand so you will know if it requires thorough fixing and cleaning.

- Tame the foliage – This tip involves cutting grasses and removing dead limbs from plants and other unnecessary and unwanted foliage hanging around the area. Ensure that all bushes and branches that tend to crowd the yard and darken its look are removed, too. Trim the hedges to make the area look neat.

- Examine the lighting fixtures – Talk to the homeowner and tell them to update the lighting fixtures. Even an investment as minor as a light for the front porch can really improve the curb appeal of the home.

However, you also have to scrutinize the other lighting fixtures in front of the house. These include the ones installed on both sides of the garage as well as the street light in the yard. Keep in mind that even if prospective buyers tend to visit and look at the property during the daytime, aesthetically pleasing lighting fixtures can still improve the curb appeal of the home even if you do not turn them on.

Most of these tips are just simple and minor changes, but they can really contribute to signing the house you are listing to its new owner.

Preparing the Interior of the Home

Again, there is no need to ask the homeowner to make major improvements in the home's interiors. A simple preparation involving rearrangement, minor repainting, and thorough cleaning can already help. One reminder for clients who intend to sell their homes is that there are times when the house shows will be scheduled without a lot of advanced notice.

Because of that, it is necessary to maintain the spotlessness of the home once you have already listed it for sale. Ensure that the house is fully prepared for showing, especially its interiors, every time someone contacts you. The following are just simple preparation tips that can make a huge difference in the home's interiors:

- Do a thorough cleaning regularly – Vacuum or hard mop floors, steam carpets, polish appliances, and clean the windows. You also have to schedule the regular scrubbing of the bathrooms. By doing that, you can help preserve the pristine condition of the home until you have successfully transferred it to the buyer.

- Declutter – Ask the homeowner to declutter, too. Every room should be free of any item that may clutter the space and make it look smaller. Make it a point to depersonalize, as well. The homeowner should remove all personalized décor and family pictures in the home.

Keep in mind that when showing the interiors, your goal is to make the prospective buyers visualize themselves living in the house. You can't expect them to picture that if there are still personalized items and family pictures hanging on the wall.

- Rearrange furniture items – If there are furniture items, remove the unnecessary ones, particularly those that only crowd the room. You should also swap some pieces in and out of various rooms so you can give every space a clear purpose. For instance, you may want to put a compact chair and desk in a bonus room.

It may help to show prospective buyers that they can use this room as a home office.

- Clean up storage spaces – Keep in mind that the majority of those who intend to buy a home want to invest in a property with sufficient storage space. Because of that, you can expect most of them to open the closets, garage doors, pantry, and any other storage areas during the showing.

  It is therefore important to keep the storage areas as tidy as possible. Avoid showing additional and unnecessary belongings in the closets or other storage places. You have to make the area appear tidy, instead of being overfilled and crowded.

- Make the area look bright and light – You can do that by opening up all the blinds and curtains. You should allow natural light to come in. Also, leave the lights on every time you vacate for a scheduled showing.

- Do some minor repairs – Observe the interior and find out what repairs and improvements the homeowner should focus on . Some of the minor repairs that should be completed prior to showing the home are replacements for cracked floor and counter tiles. Any hole found in the walls also needs to be patched.

- Repair faucets that leak as well as drawers that jam and doors that do not close properly. Also, consider repainting the walls with neutral shades or colors. This is especially true if the present color is either purple or hot pink. Replace any damaged and burned-out lights and bulbs, too. Suggest any minor repair that the homeowner can do to make the home's interiors more appealing to the buyers.

- Accentuate the best features of the home – Before making the home available for showing to prospective buyers, identify what its best features are. This will let you know what you should accentuate or emphasize during the showing. For instance, if you feel like the beautiful hardwood floors are the best features of the property, take off the rug that covers them. That way, you can show it off to the buyers.

- Lastly, before the first showing, take time to observe every bit of detail in the interiors. Look at each room while lingering in the doorway. Visualize how it will appear to a prospective buyer. Also, do final scrutiny on how the furniture and fixtures are arranged. Rearrange some pieces, if necessary, until the home brings out its best visual appeal.

As for the window coverings, ensure that they hang evenly. After cleaning, repairing, and organizing everything, especially the interiors, you can start showing and staging the home.

Making a Great First Impression

Leaving a great first impression to prospective buyers is essential for real estate agents. It can help close a sales deal. The best thing that you can do is to show the property in the best light possible. You should impress the buyers as it can influence them visually and emotionally, thereby encouraging them to give you their best offer.

To ensure that you will not leave a bad impression on prospective buyers, never show a property until it is completely ready. Fix everything that requires fixing based using the tips mentioned earlier.

Basically, the general fix-ups in the exteriors and interiors that you should focus on are the landscaping, driveway, interior and exterior painting, carpeting, roofing, and curb appeal. Once you take care of all these things, you have a higher chance of leaving a good impression and successfully selling the house to a good buyer.

Chapter 6

Creating Ongoing Success in Real Estate Sales

To become successful as a real estate agent, you need to be able to maintain your relationships with your clients for a long time. It could be that they will always seek your service whenever they need the help of a real estate agent or refer you to the people in their circle, thereby increasing the number of your leads and prospects.

Now, the question is, how can you make that happen? How can you build ongoing success in real estate sales? This chapter will give you some ideas on what you should do to be successful in this industry for as long as you want.

Keeping Clients for Life

Your success as a real estate agent will always rely on a constant two-pronged tactic – marketing your skills and expertise to generate new leads and preserving your good relationship with your previous clients. This means that your focus should not only be on lead generation. You also have to continue communicating with your previous clients and retain that connection for life.

Fortunately, it is not that hard to do so, especially if they are among your most satisfied and happiest clients. You just have to continue reminding them that you are the top choice whenever they need the help of an agent.

Here are some things you can do to keep most, if not all, of your happy and satisfied clients for life:

Personalize Communication

One of the best ways to retain the interest of your past satisfied clients is to keep your communication as personal as possible. Note that at present, when all people are starting to get bombarded with correspondence and information, it is even more important to look for a way to remain relevant to your client.

You have to do that without sounding too intrusive. Instead of sticking to standardized or group emails, consider personalizing and customizing your messages. Your message should be something that the client can easily relate to. Your messages should also contain information that your clients will truly find useful and valuable. With this move, they will perceive you as an asset – one who they would like to keep and contact whenever they need your service.

Act as a Trusted Resource and Advisor

Focus on offering real value to your clients. The more you do that, the higher is the chance for your clients to trust you and be loyal to you. They will even start referring you to their friends and family. Continue acting as a trusted resource and advisor to your clients even after you have completed your deals.

Send them newsletters and post blogs that are creative and provide plenty of relevant market information. Provide them with articles written by property experts, too. Your goal here is to make them recognize your sales and property expertise.

They should view you as an expert in the area you are in, so avoid sending them annoying and irrelevant articles and news. Your past clients should continue viewing you as an industry expert. That way, they will continue to seek your services whenever necessary.

Be Honest

Make sure to demonstrate your honesty in everything that you do with your clients. Note that you can expect your relationship with them to be only short-lived if you are not honest with the details and information you relay to them. If they sense your dishonesty, then they will not be able to give you their full trust.

Remember that most clients nowadays are smart. They are fully aware when an agent is manipulating them. Never tarnish your reputation by lying to them and failing to deliver what you promise. You should build a reputation of integrity as this is also the key to cultivating a long-term relationship with your clients.

Establish and Show Your Strong Code of Ethics

You can actually forge a long-lasting relationship with your clients if you show them how strong your code of ethics is. While growing your business or career in the real estate industry, you should navigate it with a clear and solid set of principles that will let you operate coherently. If you do that, everyone around your circle, including your clients, will understand what to expect from you and how you function when doing your job.

Find the Value of Each Client

This means you should perceive them as more than just your clients. Avoid looking at them as just your way of earning income. Treat them as individuals and pay attention to their concerns and interests. The ultimate goal is to identify with every client as a person instead of just looking at them as an opportunity to earn money. By doing that, you can strengthen your bond, which you can continue even after you have completed the deal.

Offer Rewards to Your Most Loyal Clients

Avoid being complacent when it comes to connecting with your previous and long-term clients. Note that there are instances when real estate agents begin to focus more on acquiring new clients to the point that they already forget the ones they had before, especially those who were loyal to them.

Avoid making this mistake. There should be a balance between generating new leads and retaining the interest of your present clients. For your most loyal clients, do not forget to reward them. You can do so in the form of exclusive discounts or some unique reward program offerings. Also, express your gratitude all the time. Find new and creative ways to relay how thankful you are for their valued trust, too.

Think Long-Term When Serving Your Clients

This means exerting all effort to satisfy the needs of your clients and to make them part of your network for a long time. By doing that, you will turn into their preferred agent. You can also expect to become their valued source of repeat and new business for many years.

Creating After-the-Sale Service

Achieving ongoing success in real estate sales is also possible if you constantly create and provide after-sales service. Note that the ultimate way to test the skills, dedication, and ability of a real estate agent is to see how he is involved with the buyer and seller even after closing the sale.

Deciding to work as a real estate agent also means you need to hone your caring and supportive nature. It is what will make you realize and accept the fact that you actually have to work even harder after closing a sale than before it. Some of the after-sales services and duties you have to offer to your clients are:

- Make sure that all legal documentation, particularly the deed of sale, is already drawn up with both parties' signatures on them – This is actually the most important part of the transaction, but, in most cases, there are delays to it. The reason could be that one party starts to have doubts or difficulties or is just unavailable. You may want to butt in to ensure that this will not get delayed even further.

- Ensure compliance with all the deed of sale's financial aspects – You have to offer help to ensure that all costs and deposits, including conveyancing and transfer fees, are ready in a timely manner. Note that if this is delayed, then the whole process may be held up for longer, too.

- Ensure the timely settlement of all transfer duties and outstanding rates.

- Obtain all obligatory certificates that the seller needs to convey to the authorities – Among these certificates are those that are for water, gas, plumbing, and electrical compliance. Help ensure that nothing is missing here to prevent a delay in transfer.

- Help in the compliance of all suspensive conditions, especially those that apply to the buyer, like the sale of another property or award of a bond. If those are not achieved, then you should also be available to help by taking appropriate steps in helping the buyer agreeing to a new transaction or deal.

- Make sure that the property is in excellent condition at the specific time the new owner moves in – Do not make the mistake other agents make who tend to neglect the tidying up stage within one to two weeks before a move.

When creating your after-sales service, focus on figuring out what most of your clients specifically need. Use this as your training during the first few years of your career. Train yourself to stick to the highest standards when working as a real estate agent. Show your good code of ethics through your after-sales service, too.

Note that even services as minor as offering assistance to the new homeowner to find schools for their kids around the neighborhood can show how good you are at your job. By showing your clients that you have their welfare at heart, you can boost your credibility and make the most of your clients who will build an ongoing relationship with you.

Spend Less Time to Achieve More

Your success in real estate sales will also be ongoing if you improve your productivity. This means you should start mastering the habit of spending less time to achieve more. But how can you boost your productivity when your job as a real estate agent can make most of your days unpredictable?

The ultimate solution is to figure out how to gain complete control of your day. Remember that you can attain success in the industry only if you spend your time and day doing only meaningful and valuable work.

To help you become a more productive real estate agent, especially at the start of your career, here are some highly valuable tips:

- Keep track of your time – Also, ensure that your focus is only on a single thing at a time. Note that no matter how hard you try to do everything, it is still not ideal to multitask as it may only reduce your efficiency. Remember that your brain is hard-wired to focus only on one thing. This means that even if you try to do several things all at once, there is still a high chance that you will not be able to do them well.

  With that in mind, learn how to keep track of your time. If possible, use those time-tracking apps available at present, so you can document and find out where you spend your time every day. It is also helpful to determine how and where you can boost your productivity. It allows you to focus on just one task while gaining insights on where you should put the majority of your time so you can attain growth.

- Avoid answering spam calls – Being a real estate agent may subject you to numerous phone calls and messages every single day. Unfortunately, not all of the calls you receive are from leads or clients. As a matter of fact, a lot of them tend to come from spam calls.

Answering all these calls may affect your productivity.

One thing that you can do is to avoid spam calls as much as possible. You can do that with the help of certain apps capable of screening inbound calls. Using these, you can get rid of spam and answer only those calls that come from genuinely interested leads and clients.

- Monitor your expenses – Real estate agents are also known for having plenty of personal expenses. If you do not manage and keep track of them well, then you will also be wasting a lot of your time thinking about where you allocated your money.

  Make a habit to track all of your expenses, particularly those involving your business. Create just one system where you can monitor where your money goes. Doing so will save a lot of your time, leaving you with more to spend on discussing business with prospective clients.

- Develop the habit of waking up early – Start emulating the habit of the most successful people in the world, which is waking up early. Some millionaires even have that habit of waking up several hours before they actually begin their day. Sticking to this habit will give you plenty of time to do more tasks, which can contribute a lot if you want to become one of the top-producing agents in the real estate agent industry today.

- Use a daily planner – If you want to spend less time attaining more, then a daily planner can be your life-saver. A daily plan is necessary for all real estate agents. Without it, you will be at risk of failing.

  How often did you miss an opportunity or forget to call a prospect or lead to follow-up just because you were not able to put it in your planner or calendar? Prevent that from happening to you most of the time by ensuring that you plot out your week.

  Know exactly what you will be doing every day of the week. It can contribute a lot to your continued success in the real estate industry.

- Create a to-do list – Your creativity will also have a significant boost if you create a to-do list all the time. Start your day with this list and cross off any task that you have already accomplished. Apart from making you feel good, it can help motivate you to do a lot of things within the day. It can also help you to improve your accountability.

- Prioritize those tasks that provide the highest gains – As a real estate agent, you may be facing several conflicting priorities. Master how you can recognize and manage your priorities so you can produce better professional results. Focus on finishing those that can provide you with the most gains.

Do not get distracted by other unnecessary tasks unless the task is so quick that it will only take less than two minutes. Decide on the tasks that hold the highest promise as far as your career and business growth are concerned and stick to finishing them first.

- Limit your use of social media to only the most important tasks – Working as a real estate agent means that you can never fully abandon social media. The problem is that these networks can also be time-wasters. Learn how to manage your use of your social media accounts in the best way you can.

  You can do that by putting limits on the exact times you should be using them throughout the day. Be disciplined when sticking to the schedule, too. Start looking at social media as your tool for success in the real estate industry and not as a distraction.

By doing all these things, you can surely transform yourself into a highly productive real estate agent. These tips can even help you to manage your daily activities and get rid of your procrastination. By doing that, you can accomplish a lot of valuable tasks without spending too much time on them.

The 80:20 Rule

The 80:20 rule is a very significant principle in the lives of real estate agents. This rule states that 80 percent of your results will be derived from 20 percent of your activities. In terms of real estate sales, this ratio may be an understatement. This means that smart teams and real estate agents have to constantly remind themselves that at least 80 percent of their success comes from prospecting.

Based on that principle, try spending your time accordingly. So basically, this rule is a big contributor when it comes to managing your day-to-day activities, boosting your productivity, and preventing you from procrastinating. It is all about doing more of those tasks that will bring in more business and less of the other unnecessary stuff.

The key to make this rule a part of your life is implementation. Start focusing more on prospecting. If you are asking yourself how you can relentlessly prospect when you have a lot of things left to do, then the answer is internalizing the truth that your number one job is actually prospecting. Any other task may just serve as a distraction and interference, especially if you do not know how to manage your workload.

For you to implement the 80:20 rule in your real estate operations while making it as sales-driven as possible and without it taking over your life, you can use the following tips. The good thing about these tips is that they can also help you finish all minor and administrative tasks that are waiting for your attention.

Prioritize Prospecting

Of course, prospecting should take a huge chunk of your time and effort. If possible, block at least 25 percent of the time you spent at work for prospecting only. This means using that time only for contacting previous and prospective clients to do new business.

Prospecting, in this case, refers to direct communications with past and prospective clients. Think of using text messages and phone calls instead of just general marketing emails. Your goal should be to dedicate 25 percent of this time to generate new activity.

You should then allocate another 50 to 60 percent of your time actually selling or listing homes during your scheduled appointments with clients. If you are still new, then it is understandable if you face challenges securing a lot of appointments. Do not beat yourself up if that happens. It is actually okay, especially if you are still new to the industry.

However, you should aim to polish and hone your skills and knowledge and master how to increase the time you can spend on more profitable prospecting instead of replacing this task with soft marketing efforts and administrative tasks. Another thing that you should remind yourself of is that time blocking does not mean reserving the time. What it means is that you should avoid letting other concerns and issues take over the time you have blocked for prospecting.

Develop a Plan

Some real estate agents set aside around 80 percent of their present effort to things that are not truly productive and vital for their business. This makes it necessary to plan your day beforehand. Start setting priorities – after all, this is what the 80:20 rule wants you to apply.

Determine the most important things, particularly those that can provide you with the greatest returns. Prioritize them. By doing that, you can prevent procrastination and unnecessary interruptions from sapping your time and energy.

Set Up an Effective Task Management System

The 80:20 rule will always require you to recognize and set priorities. However, to make the most out of adhering to your priorities, it is also important to pair it up with a highly effective organizational and task management system.

Instead of just using post-it notes that will not let you go that far in terms of managing your tasks, use advanced systems and tools. That way, you can set up a highly effective task management system that will let you capitalize on the remaining 20 percent that you can allocate to other tasks and duties.

Advertise Wisely

In the real estate industry, the 80:20 rule may also apply to 80 percent of successfully closed deals resulting from 20 percent promotions and advertising. With that said, you need to improve your knowledge about the wisest ways to advertise your services. Note that while there are numerous ways to advertise your offers and services, only a few of them are truly cost-effective and productive.

For instance, while postcards and mailers are among the most effective traditional forms of advertising, many still think that it is better to capture leads through digital and online marketing, as this approach tends to reach out to more people. Apart from that, digital marketing is not as time-consuming as traditional forms of advertising. It is the reason why it is wiser to use digital marketing compared to other forms of promotion and advertising.

Work Smarter, Instead of the Longer

The 80:20 rule also teaches most real estate agents to work smarter instead of longer. You should work on what is truly valuable and profitable for your business and career. Remember that more work hours do not necessarily indicate that you are wise and effective when it comes to managing your time.

What you should do, instead, is to try spending 80 percent of your available time on the 20 percent of tasks requiring your complete attention. By doing that, you can expect other things to fall into their rightful places.

Chapter 7

Listing Presentation Strategies

When trying to leave a good impression on your leads and prospects, the way you deliver your listing presentation matters a lot. You have to leave a fantastic first impression so you can convince your target to list with you. You can do that by making your listing presentation as impressive as possible.

In this chapter, you will learn some of the most useful listing presentation tips that are sure to make you stand out and boost your chance of winning and closing a deal.

Win the Seller with Proper Planning and Preparation

One effective listing presentation strategy that you can use to obtain an edge over your other competitors while increasing your chance of winning a deal is proper planning and research. Conduct extensive research so you will learn more about not only the property but also the prospect and their motivation for selling.

The more knowledge you acquire before your scheduled presentation, the better your chance of winning it. Before you schedule your listing presentation, start building a relationship with your prospect that revolves around trust. Ask beforehand about the urgency and timeline for selling.

Ask about their actual reasons, too. If possible, inquire about the number of agents they are currently interviewing. Request an appointment, too. If you can convince them to set yours as the last appointment among the other agents, they are interviewing, that will be even better. Once you have successfully scheduled an appointment, do the necessary planning and research with the help of the following:

- Gather all relevant information about the seller and listing the property – You may want to get your hands on the property's tax records so you can check further details about the property. Your research should also include doing a quick search in Google, so you will know if your prospect has retained a strong online presence on certain networks and websites, like Facebook, Instagram, and LinkedIn.

- Drive around the neighborhood and drive by the actual property in question – Doing this allow you get a feel for what the neighborhood is like. You can also use this session to get an image or two for you to use for the actual presentation. It is crucial to have a picture of the property to improve comparative market analysis (CMA) unless the house was already listed in a multiple listing service (MLS) before.

- Find out whether the property was sold in the past – In this case, you may want to check some previous MLS records, as these will give you an idea about whether property history. If it is, then take note of its past pricing trends, as you can also use those during the presentation.

- Create a list of basic fixes and repairs for the property – The fixes should be capable of boosting the chances of the listing getting sold. It is the reason why you have to research beforehand what you think is needed to improve the property. Also, ensure that this list applies to all kinds of homes, is easy to implement, and has the ability to provide a great return on investment.

Some great examples would be:

- Repainting, especially the flaws of the present paint
- Raising shades and blinds not only to let more light in but also to make a room feel more open
- Updating the house's landscape
- Cleaning and decluttering storage areas
- Staging primary living areas

- Removing overcomplicated decors and trying to simplify them
- Replacing and repairing burned-out or broken lighting fixtures

Apart from the mentioned tips, you can also carefully and extensively plan for the listing presentation by comprehending the exact reason/s your prospect is selling. It could be that they are responding to a certain life-changing event, like the departure of their kids from college or getting a new job. Determine the exact reason as you can use it to make your listing presentation fit their unique needs.

Make sure that you also go to your scheduled appointment fully prepared. Gather everything you need for the presentation and organize yourself well, so you won't end up not knowing what to say when your prospect asks you something or request some references.

Some things you should prepare and bring to the presentation are the following:

- Most recent market trends and statistics – You may craft these details in your comparative market analysis (CMA) or print a copy from the MLS. Such information can help in backing up all your statements during the presentation.

- Appropriate marketing sheets.

- Attractive and full-color market presentation and analysis – This can help to retain the attention of your prospect.

- Graphs and other visuals for data interpretation – Such visuals should clearly show the prospects the exact position of their home or property in the market.

- A sales pitch – This should demonstrate the exact reasons why you are the perfect real estate agent for a particular prospect. Mention your area expertise, past transactions similar to this one, personal connection to the reasons your prospect is selling, and a lot more.

- Attractive and brightly designed brochures – You can leave these materials with your interested prospects.

- Your recommendations on who will be taking the pictures of the property – Bring samples of the work of this professional, too, so your prospect will be able to assess them.

In addition, you can fully prepare by knowing your exact strengths as a real estate agent. By being aware of that, you can confidently deliver your presentation because you have faith in the value of all your prepared resources as well as your expertise and knowledge.

Know Your Competition

Competition in the real estate industry is kind of steep. The same is true for real estate agents vying for the attention of potential leads and prospects. It is the reason why you have to make the most out of the opportunity to get as far as scheduling a sit-down meeting with your prospects. Begin your presentation by detailing the specific reasons why you are uniquely and better suited to represent their specific interests.

Provide specific information about what you do and the experience that makes you distinguishable from competitors. If possible, dedicate the first two slides to emphasizing the recent case studies and successes you had with your previous clients. You may also want to study your competition, so you can present whatever it is that makes you truly distinctive from them.

Also, keep these valuable tips in mind that will certainly help you stand out despite the fierce competition of real estate agents.

- Do not speak ill of other agents competing for a particular deal – Yes, there is a tough competition but fight fairly by ensuring that you do not talk badly about them. Just compete based on your skills. Talk with respect about your fellow real estate agents. You will be surprised how this simple move will receive the same level of respect and courtesy in return.

- Offer the same service regardless of the property's value – Do not limit the services you offer to prospective clients just because their properties have a lower value. You should treat them equally and fairly no matter how much their property is worth.

- Encourage prospects to interview more than just one real estate agent – Yes, you need to win this deal, but you have to show prospects that you are confident in your skills and expertise. That said, encourage them to assess the skills of different agents so they can pick the right one.

- Avoid pressuring your prospects – You can tell them what you want and request it when you successfully close the deal, but this does not mean you should pester them with incessant demands. Doing so may only cause them to look for another agent. Also, try to be someone capable of informing your prospects about the market without ending up getting pushy or aggressive.

- Be honest – Let your prospects have an honest opinion, whether it is good or bad news about the property they are planning to list. Make sure that you are constructive when relaying your advice, too. Avoid sugar-coating the situation. Let them know right away what to expect from the deal.

Ensure that you also make eye contact and smile. This is important to boost your likeability while making you look more approachable and accessible. When delivering your presentation, speak confidently and clearly. All these things can help you win over the competition.

It also helps to showcase how you have helped your previous clients to sell their properties quickly. You may also want to share how you helped them handle a challenging and tricky situation just by understanding their unique requirements and needs.

Use this specific time during the presentation to incorporate some case studies and statistics from the company you are a part of. That way, your prospects and leads will also know immediately that there is a successful and experienced team backing you up.

Use Technology to Impress Clients

You also have a higher chance of delivering your listing presentation well and gaining great results from it by making technology work for you. Let them know how well-versed you are in using technology when it comes to marketing and promotion.

One thing that you can do is update your digital assets. Update all tools that are over two months old. Note that your digital assets will serve as your behind-the-scene assistants. Your prospects can check those out before, during, and after the presentation. Your up-to-date digital assets are capable of supplementing your in-person efforts, making it all the more important to ensure that they are in fighting form.

Of course, the first thing that you should regularly update and refresh is your website. All the materials you decide to send out, including direct mail, flyers, and social media posts, need to be capable of driving significant traffic to your website. Ensure that all the details on your site are updated. They should look tidy and organized, too.

The website you share with your prospects and leads during your listing presentation should be capable of reflecting the professionalism they most likely expect from their chosen agent. Another thing to remember regarding the use of technology for your listing presentation is that software tends to evolve in just a couple of seconds.

With that said, do not forget to update any app or software you are using for your business. This is especially true for those apps you use every time you deliver your presentation. The good news is that you can now easily update apps frequently. Ensure that the most important versions of the apps and software you are using right now have the latest features, fixes, and updates.

You can also impress your clients with your adeptness in using technology to their advantage through the following:

- Provide samples of how their property will appear on social media – Let them know that part of your plan when selling their home is to use the power of social media platforms, but you have to show them how it will play out. One way to do this is to stage a listing on Facebook. You may also what to show them a few tweets you intend to send out regarding their property's open house.

- Show your prospects how the listing was optimized for mobile use – With your smartphone and tablet, demonstrate to your prospect how you intend to optimize their listing so it is viewable on all forms of mobile devices. By doing this, you can demonstrate to them that you are truly adept in technology. It also shows your full understanding of how buyers today use mobile devices in searching for homes.

- Present data in a more dynamic manner – Note that while statistics and figures are among the essential parts of your listing presentations, they are also considered the driest and most boring portions. In this case, you may want to use technology to create attention-grabbing and engaging graphics from the data.

This means that instead of the usual pyramid or pie chart, you may want to create an infographic, which can help in displaying market statistics in a unique and modern way. You may also use some reliable websites that provide themed templates where you can just drop the data and customize them with your preferred colors and fonts.

- Include a video walking tour in your presentation – Make sure that a video walking tour is part of your listing presentation. Note that a lot of home shoppers at present view the interiors of property virtually – often through videos. The good news is that you do not have to study complex coding to share videos on various online platforms. It is quick as it only involves clicking a button. Let your prospects know about that, and they will be encouraged to give your service a try.

- Give your leads/prospects access to your account on Google Drive – You should then present it to them on your mobile device so they can see how it works. Let them see how easy and quickly it is to use it for sharing information, forms, pictures, and collateral. Demonstrate how they can quickly and easily access such information, too.

All these tips can show your clients that you know exactly how to make the most of technology when selling their properties. By doing that, expect to leave a positive impression after the presentation, which may produce favorable results.

Insert Trial Closes Strategically

Trial closes are also among the most vital parts of your listing presentation. As a matter of fact, a trial closing is necessary for any sales process. Every salesperson is fully aware of how useful and important it is to gain even more information about a client and bring them closer to closing the deal or making a sale. You should, therefore, make it a part of your listing presentation.

A trial closing actually refers to a smaller close, which gives you an idea of whether your prospect is already prepared to work with you. It is softer compared to the actual close. You may want to use it to move the sale along. This is especially true if you plan to make a point once the initial segments of your presentation come to an end.

A trial close is often delivered in the form of a question. It is usually a means of engaging your prospects in the conversation and somewhat scrutinizing how they felt about any part or topic of your presentation without pressuring or pushing them too much. Some of the best questions you can insert as the most strategic trial closes in your listing presentation are:

- So, are you interested in getting started on _____ (suggest date)?
- Do you find my solution sensible?
- What do you think about the techniques and solutions we have talked about so far?
- What are your thoughts about _____ (benefit/feature of a service)?
- How do you feel about my proposal?
- When do you think is the best time for me to send the paperwork?
- Would this solution work for you? Do you think it can benefit you?

- Do you have any questions?
- Does this seem like the type of solution you were expecting?

When saying those trial closes, wait and listen carefully for their responses. Aside from carefully listening to what they say, assess how they respond to your questions, too. Also, make sure you give them a few more seconds after they provide their response. This should give them more time in case they still have other things to say.

At the end of your presentation, ask about the things that you have not covered that are important to your prospects. By using this strategy, you will know your exact position in the sales process, which will also give you a clear idea of the best steps you can take next.

When used properly, these trial closes can help you remain on a similar page as your leads and prospects, thereby giving you control over the actual sales process.

Talk About Value Instead of Price

Your listing presentation should also focus more on value instead of the price. The goal here is to let your prospects see the value of the services you offer instead of worrying about how much it will cost them. This technique requires you to sell on value to ensure that the price will no longer be a hindrance to you when closing a sale.

You can achieve that by having a meaningful conversation with your prospect and asking all the right questions so they can completely understand the problem and figure out how you can help them. It would also be best to encourage your prospect to tell you about their expected value rather than you laying it out to them. The reason is that if you let them know about your offered value, then there is a chance that they will look at it as irrelevant.

By asking your prospects the right questions, they will most likely let you know about the value that they are expecting once the problem is solved. By knowing that, your focus will be on your client's preferred value, resulting in it capturing their interest and looking at it as relevant.

Also, remind yourself constantly that listing presentations should never be about you. Yes, you need to let your prospects know how valuable your skills and expertise are, but you should not focus on your ego alone. Remember that the listing presentation is all about your client. This means you have to tailor it in such a way that it meets their needs. By customizing your presentation based on the needs of your client and the value they expect, you can forge a much better relationship with them.

Allow your prospect to talk, too. Give them enough time so they can respond to whatever it is that you have already discussed. Also, provide them with enough time to explain their expectations, especially in terms of value. Prepare to clarify questions, too, particularly those that can help you focus more on value rather than price. Ask your prospects the following:

- What do you expect regarding the timeline to sell/rent?
- Do you have an ideal listing price? What is it?

- Do you plan to work with a specific kind of buyer (ex. young couple, family, fix and flippers, or young and single professionals)?
- Would it be okay for you if I toured your property so I can assess the assets and value better?
- Does the property have any unique problem or asset?

The answers to these questions will allow you to find other valuable things to focus on regarding the property and the needs of your prospect, instead of just the price.

Be Willing to Walk Away

The way you deliver your listing presentation plays a crucial role in closing deals. However, you should know when to walk away and give up on a listing. Keep in mind that your success as a real estate agent will not be solely measured by the number of properties you have sold. It is actually all about knowing exactly what properties to sell.

This means that you can't expect all listings to be smart. As a matter of fact, it would be smarter for you not to take certain listings and just walk away. Here are those unfortunate scenarios where listings are not worth it, making it better for you to just walk away so you can save more of your time and energy for something more profitable:

- When the sellers are uncooperative – It could be that you have a really hard time gathering relevant details about the property they are planning to sell. They may also be providing you with vague and inaccurate data. If you feel like your prospective client does not cooperate with you, and at times, becomes demanding, then it would be much better for you to just walk away.

- When the clients are getting a divorce – Another red flag is probably when the potential clients you are talking to and demonstrating your listing presentation to are actually filing for a divorce. Note that many things may go wrong when working with a couple who are still going through the stages of divorcing. It could be that they may not agree on the actual price, or one party may not be willing to sell.

The entire process may turn out to be extremely uncomfortable and messy if the couple has unresolved tension and conflict between them. If you go through the process of listing the home they own, then you may end up spending too much of your time and effort managing the selling process and trying to be a mediator just in case they do not agree on something. In that case, the listing is not the ideal deal to take on.

However, remember that this does not necessarily mean you have to reject all listings based on divorce. If a couple goes through divorce but is completely amicable, then you may proceed with the listing of the property.

Still, do it with caution so you will not end up regretting your decision.

- When the homeowners owe a lot – Even if the listing looks like it has all the right elements, the property is in excellent condition, satisfied homeowners, and a fantastic market price, it may still be a good idea to just let it go instead of continuing with it. This is true if you discover that the owners actually owe a lot to the point that their financial obligation is already too close to the selling price.

  It means that the property only has a small profit margin. It may not be a good idea to push through with this type of listing, as aside from the fact that you will not be earning a stable commission, it may also be extremely stressful for you and the seller. The reason is that it may turn into a short sale, which is a very long and complicated process. With that said, think twice before accepting listings under these conditions.

Aside from the above-mentioned scenarios, you should also try to avoid overpriced real estate properties. Yes, there are sellers who, even after receiving your recommendations on prices, will ask you to substantially overprice their homes. It would be best to turn this down and just walk away, as it may cause you to gamble your reputation when the property does not achieve the interest they anticipate

Clarify Service and Next Steps

You need to end your listing presentation with your prospects getting a clear understanding of all the services you offer. You also have to be clear on the next steps that you and your prospective client will take once they decide to work with you. If you haven't received a direct reply from them after the actual presentation, then your next step would be to follow up.

However, it is advisable to stick to the 2-day rule when it comes to following up. This means that you should wait for at least 2 days or 48 hours after your listing presentation before sending your prospects a message.

Also, prepare a specific question during your follow-up call. For instance, ask about their specific concerns regarding the listing or if they are already ready to list their house. It would also be great if you take the following steps after the presentation:

- Add a personal note when following up – Avoid using a form letter, though. If possible, send your prospects a handwritten note once it is time for you to follow up.

- Put your prospect on your mailing list – Just make sure you ask for their permission first. By adding them to your mailing list, you can keep in touch with them. It is still possible to connect even if they decided to wait a while before listing their property or choosing another agent.

- Provide market updates every month via email – Make it a point to connect with your prospective clients even after your presentation by sending them market updates regularly. You can send these updates via email. It can come in the form of statistics, a newsletter, or other helpful and valuable details relevant to the listing. By doing that, your name will always be on top once they feel like they are already ready to sell.

- Send a small yet personalized gift – If possible, send a gift to your prospects. Make sure that it is personalized. It can show your prospects that you are genuinely willing to establish a good business relationship with them.

Aside from that, your next steps should involve thanking your prospective clients for the time they gave you to hear your presentation. By following these last few tips, you have a better chance of building a good rapport with your prospects, which can contribute a lot toward establishing solid relationships with them and earning their trust and loyalty.

Chapter 8

Advantages of Using Teams

Your success in the competitive real estate industry can almost be guaranteed if you decide to work with a team. As a matter of fact, it is now more common for agents in the industry to work with a team. It benefits not only the agents but also their clients.

Basically, a real estate team consists of a group of agents in the real estate industry who do not only work together but also share the commission. While the team does not need to follow a strict set of procedures, the members need to pitch in for each other to share team spirit.

If you decide to work with a team, expect your clients to contact any member of the group for help or assistance. The tasks may also be delegated. For instance, one of you may be responsible for handling phone calls from buyers, while the other will accompany buyers during home-showing tours.

Another member may also be tasked to attend home inspections, handle the process of lending, and prepare purchase offers. The role of each member is usually dependent on affinities and expertise.

Being a new real estate agent, you can also gain significant benefits from deciding to work with a team as it will let you learn the ropes in the industry. The reason is that some members may be able to provide you with sufficient training and mentoring, which is a good thing as you are still trying to grow your career.

Advantages of Working in a Real Estate Team

So what are the benefits that a real estate team can provide? Here are a few of the most recognizable ones:

Guarantees a Significant Improvement in Your Skills

Joining a real estate team is probably the best thing that you can do at the beginning of your career. It is an incredible opportunity to improve the skills and expertise needed to succeed in the industry. It allows you to gain more extensive experience with the guidance and support of those who have been in the industry for a long time.

You can even spend more time with veteran agents and learn from their experiences. Someone in the team will always be around to answer your concerns and questions and provide advice when you are dealing with difficult situations. A good real estate team can also train you as you will be doing relevant tasks, like holding open houses, finding more listing opportunities, and creating buyer lead online.

With the lead generation and creation opportunities that you can get from working with a team, you can hone a lot of skills that will transform you into a really good real estate agent. These include sales and marketing skills, negotiating skills, and time management.

Keep in mind that as a beginner in the industry, the learning curve may be steep, especially if you are unable to generate leads. An effective way to hone your skills, therefore, is to join a team with members who can provide you with loads of training and sales opportunities.

It Prevents the Development of Lone Wolf Syndrome

Those who are still starting their career as real estate agents are actually prone to developing the lone wolf syndrome. It is all about having this tendency to shoulder all the burden alone. It is common among salespeople considering the fact that there are times when sales and marketing can turn into a lonely business, particularly for those working independently.

Real estate agents are prone to this type of loneliness since this industry only has limited camaraderie. Most agents also do remote work as they are not required to go to the office during strict office hours. This makes it highly likely for you to suffer from the negative effects of lone wolf syndrome at the beginning of your career.

You can prevent that from happening if you take part in a real estate team. Here, you will be able to enjoy a culture of teamwork and camaraderie, which is extremely vital for your success. The good thing about joining a team is that it allows you to participate in something that is actually larger than yourself – that is, working as part of a community with members who aim to accomplish a business vision that is in line with their personal vision.

You will also feel good once you are part of a real estate team since you will experience a caring atmosphere within the community. This can eliminate the feeling of extreme loneliness, which may happen at the start of your career.

Extensive Lead Coverage

You can also expect to have extensive lead coverage if you join a real estate team. Note that your prospects and leads, whether buyers or sellers, can easily and quickly access real estate properties and information nowadays. They can even do it at any time of the day since they are capable of accessing information 24/7. This constant access requires you to stay connected to your email, text, phone, and business as much as you possibly can be.

There is even a risk for your time with family will get disrupted since prospects may contact you to inquire anytime. Even with it being a disruption sometimes, you need to respond to all inquiries as it can help you capture leads that you can transform into actual clients. Failing to respond to an online lead may significantly lower your conversion rate. This can be extremely stressful as you also need time to recharge and relax.

This is where your team can help. It can provide you with lead coverage opportunities regardless of whether you are a leader or a member. You will also get the chance to balance your time since someone will always be around to respond to leads. Aside from that, your team can help you to expand your sphere of influence.

You will get the chance to network effectively and meet a lot of prospective clients. The reason is that some of the leads will already have been handed to you. With the extensive lead coverage that your team can offer, you will notice a significant increase in the number of prospective clients you can communicate with.

Promotes Stability of Income

Real estate agents, regardless of whether they are beginners or veterans, are fully aware that this type of career is sometimes unstable. There are times when they have overflowing income, while there are also instances when they really have nothing.

This inconsistent cycle of income is the reason why some agents have a hard time controlling their cash flow, savings, investment, and spending. This further results in overspending, especially during those periods when their income is high, and famine and scarcity during those times when their funds are low.

By working with a team, you have a much better opportunity of stabilizing your income. You can even receive help to smooth out your income swings. Every time your performance is low, there will be members in your team who are experiencing success.

Because of that, you can still earn something. If most of the members of the team perform well in terms of producing sales, then your income can be consistently stable every month.

Provides Great Leverage

Another advantage of working with a real estate team is that it can provide you with more than enough leverage. It allows you to leverage your efforts and entire business so it can create higher income from your hard work, time, and capital.

Being a real estate agent, the best leverage you can get comes in the form of listings. You can develop good leverage if you secure a listing with all other agents having access so they can also sell it. This allows you to employ a lot of agents without the need to pay them first. You only have to pay them if they can present you with a valid offer and buyer.

Another leverage you can get from working with a team is human leverage. This refers to the possibility of making sales even if you do not exert too much effort. The reason is that all the members of the team will be working together to sell a listing. They may also use it to produce more buyers to whom they can sell other real estate properties.

With a strengthened leverage position, you get the chance to increase your sales while lowering your expenses per sale. This can further result in a higher net profit for every sale you and your team make.

Promotes Specialization

You can also benefit from working with a real estate team as it can help you master your specialization. Note that in order to succeed, you need to be aware of your own strengths. You should then hone them. This is something that you can expect from being in a team. You can improve your core skills and delegate those tasks that you are weak at to members of the team with higher competence in those areas.

This means you can improve yourself based on your specialization while learning other skills little by little. The good thing about specializing in your strengths is that it has a higher chance of yielding more favorable results. It can even help you create and nurture leads through effective follow-up and prospecting since you will be using the skills you are good at.

Allows You to Coach and Train Others

Another benefit of being part of a real estate team is that it can give you a more fulfilling experience, especially once your time comes to coach and train others. You can start mentoring others as soon as you have already attained the success you were aiming for. You can start being of help to new members of the team who are still starting to learn the ropes of the industry. It is another form of achievement since it involves helping them craft and attain the careers they are hoping for.

Conclusion

The beginning of your career as a real estate agent can be overwhelming and challenging. It is not a surprise since your job can be considered the backbone of the real estate industry. You can be a salesman, buyer's advocate, consultant, negotiator, marketer, analyst, and auctioneer, among many other tasks. You may even need to accommodate clients and respond to inquiries from new leads and prospects even during your days off and late at night.

While being a real estate agent can be overwhelming and challenging at first, learning the ropes in the industry can make it easier for you to work with different kinds of people in the long run. The only thing that you need is dedication and determination to learn and improve.

Fortunately, you are now armed with almost all of the essential tips and information that you may need to start your real estate career on a strong note. Use everything that you have learned here to handle all the challenges that you face during the first few years of your career. Eventually, you will see yourself being one of the most profitable and successful real estate agents in the industry.

References

5 awesome ways to make a great first impression on home buyers. (2020, September 28). Retrieved from Immoafrica.net website: https://www.immoafrica.net/news/first-impression-home-buyers/

5 things agents must do to fully prepare for their next listing appointment. (2014, June 3). Retrieved from Inman.com website: https://www.inman.com/next/5-things-agents-must-do-before-their-next-listing-appointment/

6 best digital marketing tips for real estate agents. (2020, April 7). Retrieved from Tweakyourbiz.com website: https://tweakyourbiz.com/business/digital-marketing/real-estate-tips

10 tips for a fierce listing presentation in a competitive market. (2018, November 20). Retrieved from Inman.com website: https://www.inman.com/2018/11/20/10-tips-for-a-fierce-listing-presentation-in-a-competitive-market/

Berlusconi, E. (2019, August 9). How to choose the best real estate company. Retrieved from Demotix.com website: https://demotix.com/how-to-choose-the-best-real-estate-company/

catraining. (2017a, April 10). These 9 tips will help you effectively show property as a real estate agent. Retrieved from Carealtytraining.com website: https://www.carealtytraining.com/real-estate-client-interactions-showing-property/

catraining. (2017b, April 17). 7 benefits of joining A real estate team. Retrieved from Carealtytraining.com website: https://www.carealtytraining.com/real-estate-agent-success-joining-a-team/

Del Gigante, M. (2019, August 27). 10 powerful ways to use Instagram for real estate marketing. Retrieved from Mdgadvertising.com website: https://www.mdgadvertising.com/marketing-insights/10-powerful-ways-to-use-instagram-for-real-estate-marketing/

Dey, A. (2021, February 2). Real Estate Phone Scripts: 4 essential phone scripts for realtors. Retrieved from Hireaiva.com website: https://www.hireaiva.com/blog/real-estate-phone-scripts/

Dwyer, S. (2016, February 24). How can real estate agents maintain client relationships after the sale? Retrieved from Rismedia.com website: http://rismedia.com/2016/02/24/how-can-real-estate-agents-maintain-client-relationships-after-the-sale/

Expert Panel. (2020, August 4). 16 essential personality traits for real estate agents. *Forbes Magazine*. Retrieved from https://www.forbes.com/sites/forbesrealestatecouncil/2020/08/04/16-essential-personality-traits-for-real-estate-agents/

Guest Post. (2018, July 18). How to use Instagram for real estates to attract your #DreamLead. Retrieved from Adespresso.com website: https://adespresso.com/blog/instagram-for-real-estates/

Helling, A. (2020, February 27). How to choose a real estate brokerage to work for. Retrieved from Rethority.com website: https://rethority.com/how-to-choose-a-real-estate-brokerage-to-work-for/

How to create Facebook real estate ads: A beginner's guide. (n.d.). Retrieved from Placester.com website: https://placester.com/real-estate-marketing-academy/how-create-facebook-real-estate-ads

How to generate leads through website. (n.d.). Retrieved from Almondsolutions.com website: https://www.almondsolutions.com/blog/how-to-generate-leads-through-website

jakegosskuehn. (2019, January 4). 77 sales prospecting and qualifying tips you can use in 2019, today. Retrieved from Webstrategyviking.com website: https://webstrategyviking.com/prospecting-and-qualifying-tips/

Kimmons, J. (n.d.). Get better at closing real estate listing presentations. Retrieved from Thebalancesmb.com website:

https://www.thebalancesmb.com/the-consulting-close-of-the-listing-presentation-2867243

L'Eplattenier, E. (2020, June 1). 17 top real estate negotiation strategies from the pros. Retrieved from Theclose.com website: https://theclose.com/real-estate-negotiation/

L'Eplattenier, E. (2021, March 22). How to set up a real estate agent Facebook page to get more leads. Retrieved from Theclose.com website: https://theclose.com/real-estate-agent-facebook-page/

Linsell, C. (2020, December 17). 24 real estate cold calling scripts and tips to conquer your fears. Retrieved from Theclose.com website: https://theclose.com/real-estate-cold-calling-scripts/

Linsell, C. (2021, March 16). The 5 best real estate lead generation websites in 2021. Retrieved from Theclose.com website: https://theclose.com/best-real-estate-lead-generation-websites/

Lyons, J. (2019, November 26). What makes a good real estate agent for home sellers. Retrieved from Zillow.com website: https://www.zillow.com/sellers-guide/what-makes-a-good-real-estate-agent/

Mburugu, C. (2020, July 13). Facebook marketing for real estate agents: 6 tips. Retrieved from Mashvisor.com website: https://www.mashvisor.com/blog/facebook-marketing-for-real-estate-agents/

Randall, S. B. (2018, June 29). 5 steps to generate referrals. Retrieved from Staceybrownrandall.com website: https://www.staceybrownrandall.com/5-steps-to-generate-referrals/

Real estate cold calling scripts: 14 tips to wow leads. (n.d.). Retrieved from Placester.com website: https://placester.com/real-estate-marketing-academy/real-estate-cold-calling-scripts

Robbers, N. (2015, September 24). 16 awesome ideas to revamp your listing presentation [SlideShare]. Retrieved from Zillow.com website:

https://www.zillow.com/agent-resources/blog/revamp-your-listing-presentation/

Siani, T. (2021, March 14). How to use local SEO to boost your real Estate business. Retrieved from Growmap.com website: https://growmap.com/local-seo-real-estate-business/

Smith, B. S., Landau, C., Hovet, S., & Rojas, N. (2016, August 17). 9 real estate marketing strategies to expand your business. Retrieved from Bplans.com website: https://articles.bplans.com/9-real-estate-marketing-strategies-to-expand-your-business/

Strozyk, K. (2021, February 1). 6 best real estate lead generation companies in 2021. Retrieved from Fitsmallbusiness.com website: https://fitsmallbusiness.com/best-real-estate-lead-generation-companies/

The 80/20 rule - ultimate time management for real estate agents - REDX. (2010, May 26). Retrieved from Theredx.com website: https://www.theredx.com/blog/the-8020-rule-ultimate-time-management-for-real-estate-agents/

The ultimate real estate SEO guide (with strategies, tips & examples). (n.d.). Retrieved from Placester.com website: https://placester.com/real-estate-marketing-academy/real-estate-local-seo-tips

Top 10 objections and the scripts to overcome them. (2016, March 3). Retrieved from Tomferry.com website: https://www.tomferry.com/blog/top-10-objections-and-the-scripts-to-overcome-them/

Top 10 traits of a good real estate agent. (n.d.). Retrieved from Kapre.com website: https://www.kapre.com/resources/real-estate/top-ten-traits-of-a-real-estate-agent/

Van Steenwyk, J. (2014, July 23). 22 prospecting tips for real estate agents. Retrieved from Marketleader.com website: https://www.marketleader.com/blog/2014/07/23/prospecting-just-do-it-and-heres-how/

VanEd. (2020, February 6). 5 Instagram marketing tips for real estate agents. Retrieved from Vaned.com website: https://www.vaned.com/blog/instagram-tips-real-estate-agents/

www.ingramcontent.com/pod-product-compliance
Lightning Source LLC
Chambersburg PA
CBHW071202210326
41597CB00016B/1648